S/NVQ Level 3

Health & Social Care

(Adults)

Yvonne Nolan

with Neil Moonie and Siân Lavers

www.heinemann.co.uk

✓ Free online support
✓ Useful weblinks
✓ 24 hour online ordering

01865 888058

Heinemann
Inspiring generations

Heinemann Educational Publishers
Halley Court, Jordan Hill, Oxford OX2 8EJ
Part of Harcourt Education

Heinemann is the registered trademark of
Harcourt Education Limited

Text © Yvonne Nolan, Neil Moonie, Sian Lavers 2005

First published 2005

10 09 08 07
10 9 8 7 6 5

British Library Cataloguing in Publication Data is available
from the British Library on request.

13-digit ISBN: 978 0 435453 73 2

Edited by Jan Doorly
Designed by Wooden Ark
Typeset by Ken Vail Graphic Design (kvgd.com)
Illustrated by Graham-Cameron Illustration (Steph Dix) and The Art Collection
(Ben Croft)

Original illustrations © Harcourt Education Limited, 2005

Cover design by Wooden Ark
Printed in China Through Phoenix Offset
Cover photo: © Getty

Acknowledgements
Every effort has been made to contact copyright holders of material reproduced
in this book. Any omissions will be rectified in subsequent printings if notice is
given to the publishers.

Contents

Acknowledgements

Expert advice and guidance was provided during the preparation of this book by: **Anne Eaton**, Associate Director of Programmes, Skills for Health; **Linda Nazarko**, NVQ trainer and assessor for the NHS; **Dee Spencer-Perkins**, independent trainer and consultant for social services with a particular interest in disability issues; **Tim Thomas** and **Denise Knight**, Leicestershire Care Development Group (Tim Thomas is a member of the TOPSS England Occupational Standards and Qualifications Committee)

The authors and publisher would like to thank the following:

All at the Fremantle Trust, especially Mark Kingham, Yvonne Peace, Lorraine McGinley and the staff and residents at Farnham Common House and Seabrook Court, for their kindness and invaluable assistance (www.fremantletrust.org)

Rachel Bunn at Lowestoft College for advice and assistance

Mencap for permission to reproduce a page from its website www.mencap.org.uk (page 268)

Crown copyright material is reproduced under Class License No. C01W0000141 with the permission of the Controller of HMSO and the Queen's Printer for Scotland

The authors and publisher would like to thank the following for permission to reproduce photographs:
Alamy, pages 20, 96, 142, 178, 263, 344
Corbis, pages 14, 235, 336
Cumulus, page 38
Getty Images, pages 75, 126, 129, 230, 275
Getty Images/Photodisc, page 317
Sally and Richard Greenhill, page 332
Harcourt Education, page 371
Harcourt Education/Gareth Boden, pages 11, 23
Harcourt Education/Trevor Clifford, page 57
Harcourt Education/Tudor Photography, page 184
David Hoffman Photo Library, page 274
Photofusion, pages 245, 323
Photonica, page 166
Shout/Alamy, page 312

All other photographs by Richard Smith

Introduction

This new edition of *Level 3 Health & Social Care* comes at a time of change in the sector. So much has happened, both in terms of new legislation, guidelines and policies and in the way that issues are approached and addressed, that some changes to the National Occupational Standards were absolutely essential. Greater regulation of the care sector has been an important factor in continuing improvement, creating higher quality services and giving better protection to vulnerable people who use the services of the sector.

The new standards reflect the changes in the profession, such as the emphasis on quality services, the focus on tackling exclusion, and the influence of the culture of rights and responsibilities. There has been a huge increase, too, in understanding in all parts of the sector, and a recognition of the satisfaction that comes from working alongside service users as partners and directors of their own care, rather than as passive receivers of services.

Those users of this book who are working towards the achievement of an S/NVQ at Level 3 will be taking on a hugely demanding, but very fulfilling job role. The standards and quality of service provision continue to rise and the demands on the workforce increase continually. It is of course those who take responsibility for their own work, or who provide support and supervision to others, who often find that the most is expected of them.

However, it is clear from feedback since the introduction of S/NVQs and the massive improvement in practice shown by those who have achieved such qualifications, that all their hard work and study have played a huge part in providing a better service for the very vulnerable people who benefit.

Not everyone reading this book will be undertaking a qualification; some will use it for reference or to keep up with new developments. I hope that the content encourages you to think and reflect on your own practice.

The revised NVQ Level 3 in Health and Social Care qualification has **eight** units: **four** mandatory units and **four** options chosen from a wide selection. In this book we have included all four mandatory units and five of the most popular option units, therefore providing a choice. For details of further units, go to the Heinemann website (see below). Each NVQ unit is presented in the same way:

- **Elements of Competence** divide the unit to make it more manageable
- **About this unit** tells you the subject matter of the unit; it also spells out the **scope** of the work and the **values** relating to the unit
- **Performance Criteria** tell you what you have to do at work to achieve the standard
- **Knowledge Specification** tells you what you need to know and understand.

You will find that this book follows the structure of the NVQ units closely and gives you the knowledge for each unit. Look out for the 'Keys to good practice', as these will help you to satisfy the Performance Criteria.

You will find a helpful glossary of terms on page 379, a list of useful references on page 381, and a grid detailing coverage of the Knowledge Specification points on page 383. For more information about learning materials and resources for S/NVQs in Health and Social Care, visit the Heinemann website at www.heinemann.co.uk/vocational and follow the links.

I wish all who use this book the very best in their future career.

Yvonne Nolan

Promote effective communication for and about individuals

Communication is all about the way people reach out to one another. It is an essential part of all relationships, and the ability to communicate well with service users, colleagues and others is a basic requirement for doing your job.

Communication is not just talking – we use touch, facial expressions and body movements when we are communicating with people personally, and there are many means of written and electronic communication in today's society.

It is important that you learn to communicate well even where there are differences in individuals' abilities and methods of communication; you will also need to be able to communicate effectively on complex and sensitive issues.

Recording information is important and serves many valuable purposes. You need to understand the significance of what you record and how it is recorded, in order to be sure that you are doing the best you possibly can for the individuals you work with.

This unit will help you to understand how all of these aspects of communication can be used in order to build and develop relationships and to improve your practice as a professional care worker.

What you need to learn

- Communication differences
- How to find out about likely communication problems
- Overcoming difficulties in communication
- Communicating about difficult issues
- Undertaking difficult, complex and sensitive communications
- How to identify the support individuals need
- Ways in which people communicate
- Barriers to communication
- Listening effectively
- Ways of receiving and passing on information
- Confidentiality
- Looking after information
- How to record information

HSC 31a Identify ways to communicate effectively

Communication differences

This element deals with communication where there are differences between the worker and an individual that can cause problems. Communication differences include:

- people speaking different languages
- either the worker or the individual having a sensory impairment
- distress, where somebody is so upset that he or she is unable to communicate
- a physical illness or disability, such as a stroke or confusion
- cultural differences.

Using appropriate language

Speaking is about much more than just passing information between people. For example, many people can speak with different degrees of formality or informality. This is called the **register** of language.

If you went to a hospital reception, you might expect the person on duty to greet you with a formal phrase, such as: 'Good morning, how can I help you?'. An informal greeting of the kind used by white males in the south-east of England might be: 'Hello mate, what's up then?' or 'How's it going?'.

It is possible that some people might prefer the informal greeting in many situations. An informal greeting could put you at ease; you might feel that the speaker is like you. But in some situations, the informal greeting might make people feel that they are not being respected.

The degree of formality or informality establishes a context. At a hospital reception you are unlikely to want to spend time making friends and chatting things over with the receptionist. You may be seeking urgent help; your expectations of the situation might be that you want to be taken seriously and put in touch with professional services as soon as possible. You might see the situation as a very formal encounter. If you were treated informally, you might interpret this as not being taken seriously, or not respected.

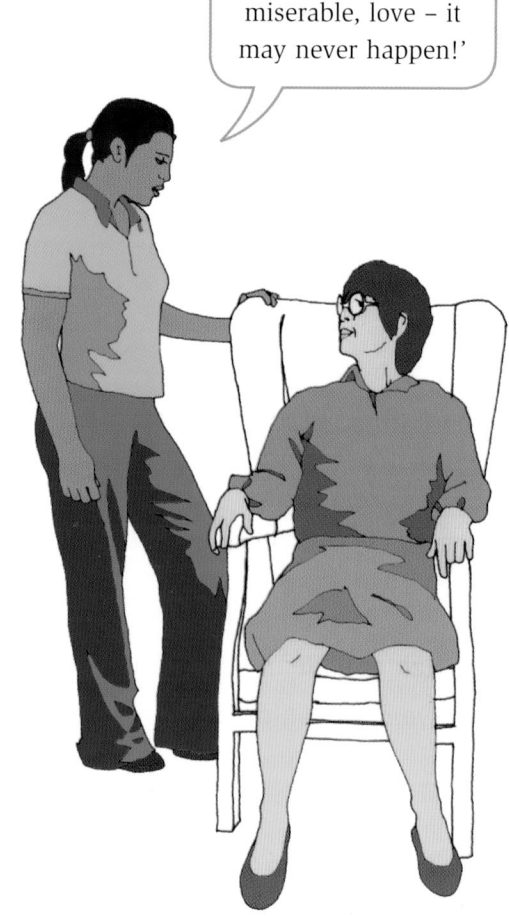

Don't look so miserable, love – it may never happen!'

Informality and informal humour may be perceived as disrespect

Styles of speaking

People from different localities, different ethnic groups, different professions and work cultures all have their own special words, phrases and speech patterns. Where communities or groups of people have particular ways of speaking we call this a **speech community**. An elderly middle-class woman is very unlikely to start a conversation with the words 'Hello mate'.

Some service users may feel threatened or excluded by the kind of language they encounter. However, merely using formal language will not solve this problem. The technical terminology used by social care workers may also create barriers for people who are not part of that speech community.

Active knowledge

> I come about getting some help around the house, you know, 'cause it's getting 'ard nowadays, what with me back an' everything.

> Well, you need to speak to the Community Domiciliary Support Liaison Officer who can arrange an assessment in accordance with our statutory obligations.

The two statements above use different levels of formality, but they also represent speech from different speech communities. Can you work out what each person is saying? How do you think the service user will feel given such a response? Will the service user feel respected and valued?

Different languages

Where an individual speaks a different language from those who are providing care, it can be an isolating and frustrating experience. The individual may become distressed and frightened as it is very difficult to establish exactly what is happening and he or she is not in a position to ask or to have any questions answered. The person will feel excluded from anything happening in the care setting and will find making relationships with care workers extremely difficult. There is the possibility that misunderstanding will occur.

People communicate differently, but establishing good communication is vital

Hearing loss

A loss or reduction of ability to hear clearly can cause major differences in the ability to communicate.

Communication is a two-way process, and it is very difficult for somebody who does not hear sounds at all or hears them in a blurred and indistinct way to be able to respond and to join in. The result can be that people become withdrawn and feel very isolated and excluded from others around them. This can lead to frustration and anger. People may present some quite challenging behaviour.

Profound deafness is not as common as partial hearing loss. People are most likely to suffer from loss of hearing of certain sounds at certain volumes or at certain pitches, such as high sounds or low sounds. It is also very common for people to find it difficult to hear if there is background noise – many sounds may jumble together, making it very hard to pick out the voice of one person. Hearing loss can also have an effect on speech, particularly for those who are profoundly deaf and are unable to hear their own voices as they speak. This can make communication doubly difficult.

Keys to good practice: Hearing impairments

When communicating with people with hearing impairments:

- ✓ make sure the person can see you clearly
- ✓ face both the light and the person at all times
- ✓ include the person in your conversation
- ✓ do not obscure your mouth
- ✓ speak clearly and slowly – repeat if necessary, or rephrase your words
- ✓ do not shout into a person's ear or hearing aid
- ✓ minimise background noise
- ✓ use your eyes, facial expressions and hand gestures, where appropriate.

(Points adapted from Hayman, 1998.)

Visual impairment

Visual impairment causes many communication difficulties. Not only is an individual unable to pick up the visual signals which are being given out by someone who is speaking, but, because he or she is unaware of these signals, may also fail to give appropriate signals in communication. This lack of non-verbal communication and lack of ability to receive and interpret non-verbal communication can lead to misunderstandings about a person's attitudes and behaviour. It means that communications can easily be misinterpreted, or it could be thought that he or she is behaving in an inappropriate way.

For people with limited vision it may be important to use language to describe things that a sighted person may take for granted, such as non-verbal communication or the context of certain comments. Touch may be an important aspect of communication; some registered blind people can work out what you look like if they can touch your face in order to build an understanding of your features.

Physical disability

Depending on the disability, this can have various effects. People who have suffered strokes, for example, will often have communication difficulties such as dysphasia – a problem with finding the right words or interpreting the meanings of words said to them. This condition is very distressing for the individual and for those who are trying to communicate. Often this is coupled with a loss of movement and a difficulty in using facial muscles to form words.

In some cases, the communication difficulty is a symptom of a disability. For example, many people with cerebral palsy and motor neurone disease have difficulty in controlling the muscles that affect voice production, and speaking in a way which can be readily understood becomes very difficult. Other disabilities may have no effect at all upon voice production or the thought processes that produce spoken words, but the lack of other body movements may mean that non-verbal communication may be difficult or not what you would expect.

Remember

Communication differences can result as much from differences in attitude as they can from differences in language or abilities.

Learning disabilities

These may, depending on their severity, cause differences in communication in terms of the level of understanding of the individual and his or her ability to respond appropriately to any form of communication. This will vary depending on the degree of learning disability of the individual, but broadly the effect of learning disabilities is to limit the ability of an individual to understand and process information given to him or her. It is also likely that individuals will have a short attention span, so this may mean that communications have to be repeated several times or perhaps paraphrased in an appropriate form. It will be very important to use words and phrases that the service user is familiar with.

Dementia/confusion

This condition is most prevalent in older people and the most common type is caused by Alzheimer's disease. People with Alzheimer's can ultimately lose the ability to communicate, but in the early stages it involves short-term memory loss to the extent of being unable to remember the essential parts of a conversation or a recent exchange.

People with memory disorders often substitute inappropriate words. A 90-year-old service user may say: 'My mother visited me yesterday'. On the surface, such

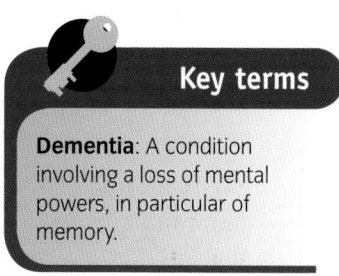

Key terms

Dementia: A condition involving a loss of mental powers, in particular of memory.

a statement appears to be irrational. From a care perspective it is very important not to challenge the rationality of what is being said; the most important thing is to make the older person feel valued and respected. Perhaps you know that the visitor was in fact, a daughter, and the service user has simply used an incorrect word. The important thing is that the service user feels safe and respected.

Sometimes a service user may be disorientated and make statements about needing to go to work or to go home to look after the children. Once again, it is important not to argue, but rather to try to divert the conversation in a way that interests and values the person. For example:

Service user: I must go home and get the tea ready for my children.

Care worker: All right, shall we walk to your room, then? You might want your coat.

Service user: Yes, that's right, you're so kind.

Care worker [now in service user's room]: Is this photograph of your son and daughter?

Service user: Yes, that's right.

Care worker: They've both got married now – aren't they both grown up?

Service user: Yes, I'm very proud of them – they're coming to visit me tomorrow.

Care worker: That's wonderful. Why don't we go downstairs and have a cup of tea?

Service user: Yes, that would be very nice – you're so kind to me.

In the exchange above, the care worker has avoided arguing about logic, and instead has gently helped the service user to remember the age her children are now. Throughout the conversation, the care worker has shown respect for the service user.

The most important aspect of communication is to show that you value and respect individuals

Cultural differences

People's communication differences can result from differences in culture and background. Culture is about more than language – it is about the way that people live, think and relate to each other. In some cultures, for example, children are not allowed to speak in the presence of certain adults. Other cultures do not allow women to speak to men they do not know.

Some people may have been brought up in a background or in a period of time when challenging authority by asking questions was not acceptable. Such people may find it very hard to ask questions of doctors or other health professionals and are unlikely to feel able to raise any queries about how their care or treatment should be carried out.

It is important to be able to identify the different interpretations that words and body language can have in different cultures. This is not a straightforward issue; words and signs can mean different things depending on their context.

Did you know?

The word 'wicked', for example, can have different meanings. If an older person used this phrase to describe his or her experience of the Second World War, the phrase would mean 'horrific' or 'terrible'. In a TV comedy from 15 years ago, the phrase would mean 'cool' – something very desirable. In a religious context, 'wicked' might relate to the concept of sin.

Taking account of context

Making sense of spoken language requires knowledge of the context and intentions of the speaker. Understanding **non-verbal communication** involves exactly the same need to understand the circumstances and cultural context of the other person. For example, in Britain the hand gesture with palm up and facing forwards means: 'Stop, don't do that.' In Greece it can mean 'You are dirt' and is a very rude gesture.

Communication is always influenced by cultural systems of meaning, and different cultures interpret body language differently. An almost infinite variety of meanings can be given to any type of eye contact, facial expression, posture or gesture. Every culture develops its own special system of meanings. Care workers have to understand and show respect and value for all these different systems of sending messages.

No one can learn every possible system of non-verbal communication, but it is possible to learn about the ones used by people you are working with. This can be done first by noticing and remembering what others do – the non-verbal messages they are sending. The next step is to make an intelligent guess about the messages the person is trying to give you. Finally, check your understanding (your guesses) with the person.

Key terms

Non-verbal communication: A way of communicating without words, through body language, gestures, facial expression and eye contact.

Keys to good practice: Skilled communication

Skilled communication involves:

✓ watching other people

✓ remembering what they do

✓ guessing what words and actions mean and then checking your guesses with the person

✓ never relying on your own guesses, because these might turn into assumptions

✓ understanding that assumptions can lead to discrimination – see Unit HSC 35.

Imagine you are working with an older person. Whenever you start to speak to her she always looks at the floor and never makes eye contact. Why is this?

Your first thought is that she might be depressed. Having made such an assumption, you might not want to talk to her. But instead, you could ask: 'How do you feel today? Would you like me to get you anything?' By checking what she feels, you could test your own understanding. She might say she feels well and is quite happy, and then request something you could do for her. This suggests that she cannot be depressed.

Then you would need to consider why else someone would look at the floor rather than at you.

Effects of communication differences

The most common effect of communication differences is for the person receiving care to feel frustrated and isolated. It is an important part of your job to do everything in your power to reduce the effect of communication differences and to try to lessen the feelings of isolation and frustration that people experience.

Evidence indicator

Try this with your colleagues. When you speak to someone, avoid eye contact and turn your head away from the person you are speaking to. What effect does this have? How does it make you feel? Make notes on your conclusions for your portfolio.

How to find out about likely communication problems

You can discover likely communication problems by simply observing an individual. You can find out a great deal about how a person communicates and what the differences are between his or her way of communicating and your own.

Observation should be able to establish:

- which language is being used
- if the service user experiences any hearing difficulties or visual impairment
- if there is any physical illness or disability
- if there is a learning disability.

Any of these factors could have a bearing on how well a person will be able to communicate with you, and what steps you may need to take to make things easier. Observation will give you some very good clues to start with, but you should work with the individual to establish exactly what is needed to assist communication. You may also consider:

- discussing with colleagues who have worked with the individual before and who are likely to have some background information and advice
- consulting other professionals who have worked with the individual and may have knowledge of means of communication which have been effective for them
- reading previous case notes or case histories
- finding out as much as you can about an individual's particular illness or disability, where you have been able to establish this – the most useful sources of information are likely to be the specialist agencies for the particular condition
- talking to family or friends. They are likely to have a great deal of information about what the differences in communication are for the individual. They will have developed ways of dealing with communication, possibly over a long period of time, and are likely to be a very useful source of advice and help.

How to record information

There would be little point in finding out about effective means of communication with someone and then not making an accurate record so that other people can also communicate with that person.

You should find out your employer's policy on where such information is to be recorded – it is likely to be in the service user's case notes.

Be sure that you record:

- the nature of the communication differences

- how they show themselves
- ways which you have found to be effective in overcoming the differences.

Information recorded in notes may look like this:

Communication plan for Mr Groves

Mr Groves has communication difficulties following surgery to remove a tumour from his tongue. His speech is slurred, but possible to understand with care. He is inclined to get frustrated when he cannot make himself understood.

Recommended actions:

- involve his key worker, Jessie, in information exchanges where possible
- provide communication flashcards to help him communicate
- ensure key conversations take place on a one-to-one basis, especially when providing information
- his own room is the best place for communication
- in the dining room, seat him by the window where it is quieter.

 Keys to good practice: Communicating effectively

✓   Check what the differences in communication are.

✓   Remember they can be cultural as well as physical.

✓   Work with individuals to understand their preferred methods of communication and language.

✓   Use all possible sources to obtain information and advice where you have difficulty communicating.

Overcoming difficulties in communication

Language differences

Where you are in the position of providing care for someone who speaks a different language from you, it is clear that you will need the services of an interpreter for any serious discussions or communication.

- Your work setting is likely to have a contact list of interpreters.
- Social services departments and the police have lists of interpreters.

Evidence indicator

Think of a service user you have worked with who has communication difficulties. Write notes that would be useful for your colleagues, describing:

- the communication difficulties involved
- the approaches you use to promote effective communication.

Keep your notes for your portfolio.

- The embassy or consulate for the appropriate country will also have a list of qualified interpreters.

You should always use professional interpreters wherever possible. It may be very tempting to use other members of the family – very often children have excellent language skills – but it is inappropriate in most care settings. This is because:

- their English and their ability to interpret may not be at the same standard as a professional interpreter, and misunderstandings can easily occur
- you may wish to discuss matters which are not appropriate to be discussed with children, or the individual may not want members of his or her family involved in very personal discussions about health or care issues.

It is unlikely that you would be able to have a full-time interpreter available throughout someone's period of care, so it is necessary to consider alternatives for encouraging everyday communication.

Be prepared to learn words in the individual's language which will help communication. You could try to give the person some words in your language if he or she is willing and able to learn them.

There are other simple techniques that you may wish to try which can help basic levels of communication. For example, you could use flashcards or sign language, as you would for a person who has suffered a stroke.

Sign language and gestures can help with basic levels of communication

The suggestions shown on the previous page are not exhaustive and you will come up with many which are appropriate for the individual and for your particular care setting. They are a helpful way of assisting with simple communication and allowing people to express their immediate physical needs.

The most effective way of communicating with a person who speaks a different language is through non-verbal communication. A smile and a friendly face are understood in all languages, as are a concerned facial expression and a warm and welcoming body position.

However, be careful about the use of gestures – gestures which are acceptable in one culture may not be acceptable in all. For example, an extended thumb in some cultures would mean 'great, that's fine, OK', but in many cultures it is an extremely offensive gesture. If you are unsure which gestures are acceptable in another culture, make sure that you check before using any which may be misinterpreted.

 CASE STUDY: A universal language

A Russian teacher accompanied a group of students on a visit to England. All of the party were staying with host families and the teacher was placed with a woman of similar age (early forties) who was a single parent with a teenage son. Neither woman spoke any of the other's language.
On the first morning the organiser of the trip spoke to the host family on the telephone and asked how the two women had got on the previous evening. He was amazed to be told that, despite not speaking a word of each other's language, they had spent the evening sitting either side of the fire with a bottle of wine and that both knew each other's life stories. They had managed to tell each other of their marriages, divorces and problems with their children. They had laughed and cried together, and had achieved all of this by using family photographs, gestures and facial expressions, and by speaking in their own language had managed to communicate their entire life histories. The two women had ended the evening firm friends and this continued throughout the rest of the visit.

1 *How do you think the women managed to communicate?*

2 *What methods of communication would you have used if you were in that situation?*

3 *Do you think it is significant that they were both middle-aged women with no disabilities? Why?*

4 *Can you think of a situation in your workplace which has any similarities to this?*

Hearing difficulties

- Ensure that any means of improving hearing which an individual uses, for example a hearing aid, is working properly and is fitted correctly, that the batteries are working, that it is clean and that it is doing its job properly in terms of improving the individual's hearing.
- Ensure that you are sitting in a good light, not too far away and that you speak clearly, but do not shout. Shouting simply distorts your face and makes it more difficult for a person with hearing loss to be able to read what you are saying.

- Be prepared to write things down if the service user prefers you to do this in order to communicate clearly.

Some people may be able to lip read, while many will use a form of sign language for understanding. This may be BSL (British Sign Language). The British Deaf Association states that BSL is a first or preferred language for nearly 70,000 people in the UK. Some deaf people may use MAKATON, a system for developing language that uses speech, signs and symbols to help people with learning difficulties to communicate and to develop their language skills. It may involve speaking a word and performing a sign using hands and body language. There are a large range of symbols that may help people with a learning difficulty to recognise an idea or to communicate with others.

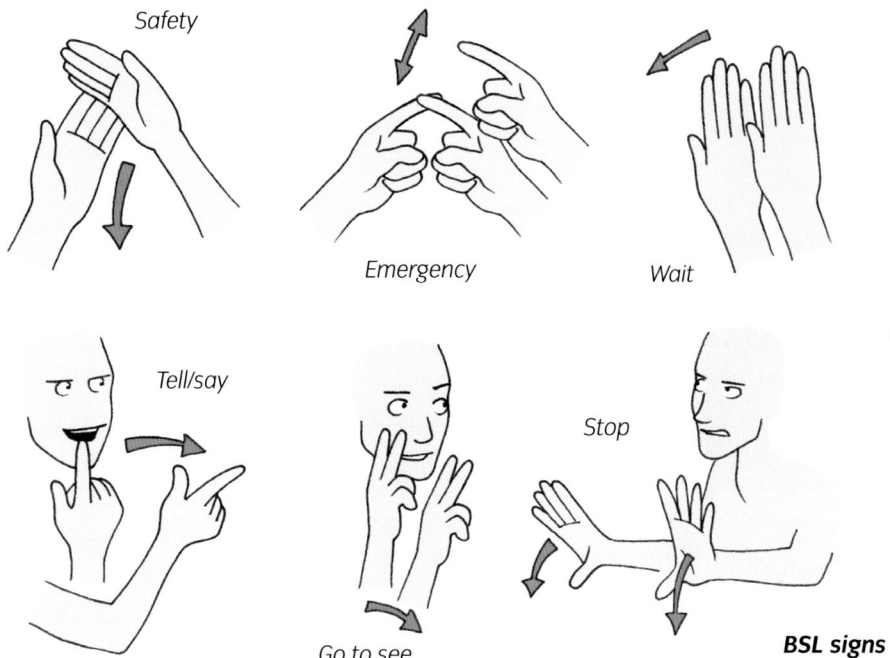

Safety

Emergency

Wait

Tell/say

Go to see

Stop

BSL signs

Remember

If you are able to learn even a few signs relevant to people who are deaf, you will significantly improve the way in which they are able to relate to you.

Other services which are extremely helpful to people who have hearing difficulties are telecommunication services, such as using a minicom or typetalk service. These allow a spoken conversation to be translated in written form using a form of typewriter, and the responses can be passed in the same way by an operator who will relay them to the hearing person. These services have provided a major advance in enabling people who are hard of hearing or profoundly deaf to use telephone equipment. For people who are less severely affected by hearing impairment, there are facilities such as raising the volume on telephone receivers to allow them to hear conversations more clearly.

Visual difficulties

One of the commonest ways of assisting people who have visual impairment is to provide them with glasses or contact lenses. You need to be sure that these are clean and that they are the correct prescription. You might advise older people to have their eyes tested every year, in order to check for diseases such as glaucoma. Younger people might be advised to have their eyes checked every two years. A person whose eyesight and requirements for glasses have changed will obviously have difficulty in picking up many of the non-verbal signals which you will be giving out when you are communicating with him or her.

For people with more serious loss or impairment, you will need to take other steps to ensure that you minimise the differences that will exist in your styles of communication.

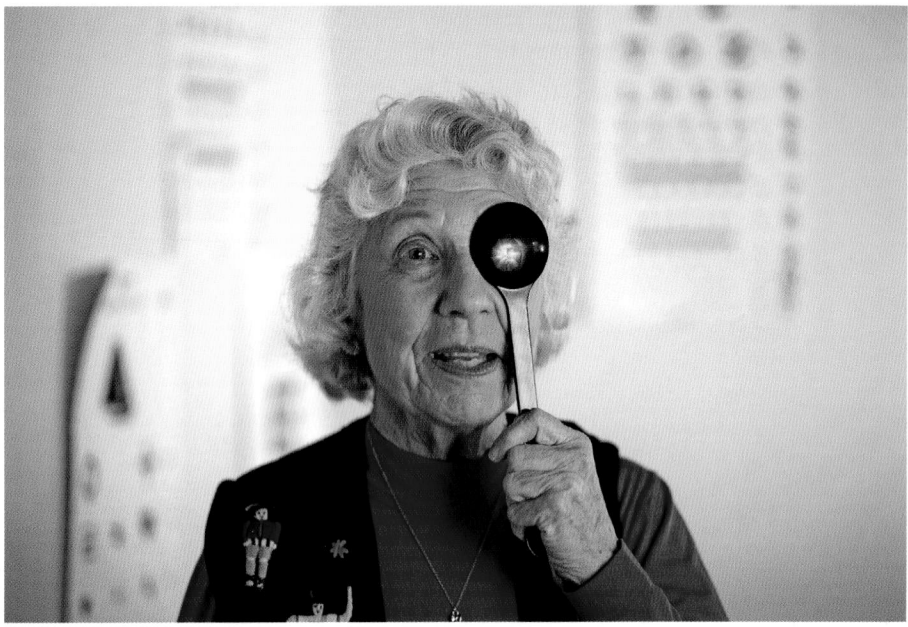

People should have their eyes tested regularly in order to check their prescription and health

 Keys to good practice: Communicating with people who have visual impairment

✓ Do not suddenly begin to speak to someone without first of all letting him or her know that you are there. One way to do this is to touch him or her, but check that the service user is comfortable with this approach.

✓ Make sure that you introduce yourself when you come into a room. It is easy to forget that someone cannot see. A simple 'hello John, it's Sue' is all that is needed so that you don't 'arrive' unexpectedly.

✓ You may need to use touch more than you would in speaking to a sighted person, because the concerns that you will be expressing through your face and your general body movements will not be seen. So, if you are expressing concern or sympathy, it may be appropriate to touch someone's hand or arm, at the same time that you are saying you are concerned and sympathetic.

Continued

✓ Ask the individual what system of communication he or she requires – do not impose your idea of appropriate systems on the person. Most people who are visually impaired know very well what they can and cannot do, and if you ask they will tell you exactly what they need you to do.

✓ Do not decide that you know the best way to help. Never take the arm of someone who is visually impaired to help him or her to move around. Allow the person to take your arm or shoulder, to ask for guidance and tell you where he or she wishes to go.

Physical disabilities

Physical disability or illness has to be dealt with according to the nature of the disability or the illness. For example, if you were communicating with someone who had a stroke you would have to work out ways of coping with his or her dysphasia (speech difficulties). This is best dealt with by:

- using very simple, short sentences, speaking slowly and being prepared to wait while the individual processes what you have said and composes a reply
- using gestures – they are helpful in terms of making it easier for people to understand the ideas you are trying to get across
- using drawing, writing or flashcards to help understanding
- using very simple, closed questions which only need a 'yes' or 'no' answer. Avoid long, complicated sentences with interrelated ideas. For example, do not say: 'It's getting near tea time now, isn't it? How about some tea? Have you thought about what you would like?' Instead, say: 'Are you hungry? Would you like fish? Would you like chicken?' and so on, until you have established what sort of meal the individual would prefer.

Other illnesses, such as motor neurone disease or cerebral palsy, can also lead to difficulties in making speech, although not in understanding it.

- The individual will understand perfectly what you are saying to him or her but the difficulty will be in communicating with you.
- There is no need for you to speak slowly, although you will have to be prepared to allow time for a response owing to the difficulties that the individual will have in producing words.
- You will have to become familiar with the sound of the individual's voice and the way in which he or she communicates. It can be hard to understand people who have illnesses which affect their facial, throat or larynx muscles.

Learning disabilities

Where people have a learning disability, you will need to adjust your methods of communicating to take account of the level of disability that they experience. You should have gathered sufficient information about the individual to know the level of understanding that he or she has – how simply and how often you need to explain things and the kinds of communication which are likely to be the most effective.

Many people with a learning disability respond well to physical contact and are able to relate and communicate on a physical level more easily than on a verbal level. This will vary between individuals and you should be prepared to use a great deal of physical contact and hugs when communicating with people who have a learning disability.

Cultural differences

Communication is about much more than words being exchanged between two people – it is influenced by a great many factors. The way in which people have been brought up and the society and culture that they live in has a great effect on the way in which they communicate.

For example, some cultures use gestures or touch much more than others. In some cultures it is acceptable to stand very close to someone, whereas in others people feel extremely uncomfortable if others stand too close. You need to find out about the person's background when you are thinking about how you can make communication work for him or her.

To find out the information you need, ask the individual if possible, and/or:
- look in the person's records
- speak to a member of the family or a friend, if this is possible
- ask someone else from the same culture, either a colleague or through the country's cultural representatives (contact the embassy or consulate and ask for the information) – alternatively you could try a local multicultural organisation
- use reference books, if necessary.

It is also important that you communicate with people at the correct intellectual level. Make sure that you communicate with them at a language level which they are likely to understand, but not find patronising. For example, older people and people who have disabilities have every right to be spoken to as adults and not patronised or talked down to. One of the commonest complaints from people with physical disabilities is that people will talk to their carers about them rather than talk to them directly – this is known as the 'does he take sugar' approach.

When you provide care for someone, you will get to know and talk to him or her, and a relationship will grow. This is not easy with all individuals you care for. When there appears to be little communication, you may find that forming a relationship is difficult.

Stages of an interaction

Communication between individuals in called an 'interaction'. As you spend time in communication with someone, the nature of the interaction will go through changes.

- *Stage 1:* Introduction, light and general. At first, the content of the communication may be of little significance. This is the stage at which both parties decide whether they want to continue the discussion, and how comfortable they feel. Body language and non-verbal communication are very important at this stage.

Body language and non-verbal communication are always important

- *Stage 2:* Main contact, significant information. The middle of any interaction is likely to contain the 'meat', and this is where you will need to use active listening skills to ensure that the interaction is beneficial.
- *Stage 3:* Reflect, wind up, end positively. People often have the greatest difficulty in knowing how to end an interaction. Ending in a positive way where all participants are left feeling that they have benefited from the interaction is very important. You may find that you have to end an interaction because of time restrictions, or you may feel that enough has been covered – the other person may need a rest, or you may need a break!

At the end of an interaction you should always try to reflect on the areas you have covered, and offer a positive and encouraging ending, for example: 'I'm glad you've talked about how unhappy you've been feeling. Now we can try to work at making things better.'

Even if the content of an interaction has been fairly negative, you should encourage the individual to see the fact that the interaction has taken place as being positive in itself.

If you are called away before you have had a chance to properly 'wind up' an interaction with an individual, make a point of returning to end things in a positive way. If you say 'I'll be back in a minute', make sure that you do go back.

Communication with service users

The principles of good communication are an important part of making sure that the individual is fully involved in dealing with any issues or difficult situations. The impact of dealing with situations in a way which makes people feel valued is enormous. Often the steps are small and do not take a great deal of effort or demand major changes – but the results are so effective that any effort you have made will be repaid many times over by the positive benefits for the individuals you care for.

CASE STUDY: Service users' beliefs

Hafsah is from Somalia in Africa and is a devout Muslim. She had her first baby in hospital in the UK. Following the delivery, Hafsah refused to get out of bed, and would press the buzzer every time she wanted anything, including asking staff to take her baby from the cot and give him to her to feed. This was in accordance with her own culture in which a new mother remains in bed for ten days after giving birth. During that time everything is done for her and her baby, and all she does is feed the baby. It is usually her mother-in-law or another female relative who takes control during this time.

The ward staff became resentful of the demands that Hafsah was making. They were not always as pleasant as they might be when they were called into her room. Hafsah became very distressed and was agitated and nervous each time she needed assistance. She began to have problems feeding the baby. There was a great deal of concern about this and about her refusal to get out of bed, and she was encouraged to do so. The midwives explained to her that she ran the risk of thrombosis or other circulatory problems if she continued to lie in bed.

A solution was eventually found by allowing her mother-in-law to remain with her in a side room to provide the care needed. But Hafsah could still not be persuaded to get out of bed. As she had been provided with all the information about possible consequences, and she had made an informed choice consistent with her own beliefs, her decision to stay in bed had to be respected.

1 *What were the issues presented by Hafsah's beliefs?*

2 *Do you think the situation was handled correctly?*

3 *What would you have done?*

Keys to good practice: Communicating on difficult or complex issues

✓ Arrange the immediate environment to ensure privacy, make communication easier and aid understanding.

✓ Check that individuals have the appropriate support to communicate their views and preferences.

✓ Use styles and methods of communication that are appropriate to the individual and the subject matter.

✓ Give individuals sufficient time to understand the content of the communication.

✓ Observe and respond appropriately to their reactions.

Life stages and development

One of the most significant influences on communication and the way people deal with difficult or stressful issues is the life stage they are at. The chart below will help you to understand the life stages service users are either at, or have experienced.

	Intellectual/cognitive	Social/emotional	Language	Physical
Infant, birth–1 year	Learns about new things by feeling with hands and mouth objects encountered in immediate environment	Attaches to parent(s), begins to recognise faces and smile; at about 6 months begins to recognise parent(s) and expresses fear of strangers, plays simple interactive games like peekaboo	Vocalises, squeals, and imitates sounds, says 'dada' and 'mama'	Lifts head first then chest, rolls over, pulls to sit, crawls and stands alone. Reaches for objects and rakes up small items, grasps rattle
Toddler, 1–2 years	Extends knowledge by learning words for objects in environment	Learns that self and parent(s) are different or separate from each other, imitates and performs tasks, indicates needs or wants without crying	Says some words other than 'dada' and 'mama', follows simple instructions	Walks well, kicks, stoops and jumps in place, throws balls. Unbuttons clothes, builds tower of 4 cubes, scribbles, uses spoon, picks up very small objects

Continued

	Intellectual/cognitive	Social/emotional	Language	Physical
Pre-school, 2–5 years	Understands concepts such as tired, hungry and other bodily states, recognises colours, becomes aware of numbers and letters	Begins to separate easily from parent(s), dresses with assistance, washes and dries hands, plays interactive games like tag	Names pictures, follows directions, can make simple sentences of two or three words, vocabulary increases	Runs well, hops, pedals tricycle, balances on one foot. Buttons clothes, builds tower of 8 cubes, copies simple figures or letters, for example 0, begins to use scissors
School age, 5–12 years	Develops understanding of numeracy and literacy concepts, learns relationship between objects and feelings, acquires knowledge and understanding	Acts independently, but is emotionally close to parent(s), dresses without assistance, joins same-sex play groups and clubs	Defines words, knows and describes what things are made of, vocabulary increases	Skips, balances on one foot for 10 seconds, overestimates physical abilities. Draws person with 6 parts, copies detailed figures and objects
Adolescent, 12–18 years	Understands abstract concepts like illness and death, develops understanding of complex concepts	Experiences rapidly changing moods and behaviour, interested in peer group almost exclusively, distances from parent(s) emotionally, concerned with body image, experiences falling in and out of love	Uses increased vocabulary, understands more abstract concepts such as grief	May appear awkward and clumsy while learning to deal with rapid increases in size due to growth spurts

Continued

- they are reacting to the behaviour of others towards them
- they are responding to something that they have heard, seen or read in the media
- they are in an environment that they find frustrating or restricting
- they are in an environment that they find intensely irritating, e.g. it is noisy or they are unable to find any personal space
- they are deprived of information and are fearful
- they have full information about a situation and they remain fearful of it
- they are anxious about a forthcoming event
- they are unable to achieve the objectives they have set themselves.

These are some of the more common triggers for distress. Clearly there are many others which you may come across depending on the setting in which you work.

Everyone has a breaking point

Active knowledge

Identify six potential triggers for distress which relate to your own work setting.

How to identify when someone is becoming distressed

When you have a close working knowledge of an individual's behaviour over a period of time it becomes easy to identify when he or she is becoming distressed. You will find that you have become 'tuned-in' to individual behaviour and can recognise the small signs that indicate a change in mood. However, you will not always know your service users so well. Also, you may have to deal with distress not only in a service user, but also in a carer or a work colleague.

There are some general indications that an individual is becoming distressed which you can use in order to take immediate action. You are most likely to notice:

- changes in **voice** – it may be raised or at a higher pitch than usual
- changes in **facial expression** – this could be scowling, frowning, snarling
- changes in **eyes** – pupils could be dilated and eyes open wider
- **body language** would demonstrate agitation and people may adopt an aggressive stance, leaning forwards with fists clenched
- the **face and neck** are likely to be reddened
- there may be excessive **sweating**
- people's **breathing patterns** may change and they may breathe faster than normal.

You are likely to notice a significant change in normal behaviour when someone is becoming distressed. For example, someone who is normally talkative may become quiet and someone who is normally quiet may start to shout or talk very quickly. Other examples are someone who is normally lively becoming still and rigid, or someone who is normally relaxed starting to walk around waving his or her arms.

You need to be aware of changes in normal behaviour even if they are far less extreme than these examples. Sometimes a subtle change in behaviour can indicate someone is becoming distressed, and you are far more likely to notice subtle changes in individuals, colleagues or carers whom you know well and have worked with over a period of time.

CASE STUDY: Signs of distress

Liz is an elderly lady who has been in a residential home for the past three years. Like most of the residents she has her own chair and she likes to sit in a corner of the main lounge. Liz is normally bright and chatty and talks happily with the staff and other residents.

As with many residential settings there is a regular influx of new residents, who usually adapt to the setting extremely well. However, the previous week a new resident was admitted who, like Liz, was very talkative and friendly, but she would continue to talk at great length and quite loudly for long periods of time. For the first couple of days Liz appeared to join in and respond to the new lady's conversation, but staff noticed she gradually responded less and less and appeared to be becoming more unhappy. One morning a staff member went into the lounge, where the new lady was talking as usual, and noticed that Liz was sitting in her corner with her head down but bolt upright in her chair with her arms bent and fists clenched, and breathing faster than usual. When the staff member crouched down to talk to Liz she noticed she had bright red cheeks.

1 *What conclusions would you reach about Liz's state of mind from looking at the physical indications?*

2 *What would be the next step you would take?*

3 *What are the potential responses from Liz?*

4 *What would be a satisfactory outcome?*

Undertaking difficult, complex and sensitive communications

If individuals are upset as the result of an outside event, such as the death of a close friend or relative, or because they have received some other bad news, there is probably little you can do to prevent the distress but the way you communicate with them on the topic and the way you handle the situation can often reduce it.

You must be careful not to pressurise individuals to discuss more than they want to. You could also offer them a choice of talking to another member of staff or a relative or friend, if they appear to be unwilling to discuss their worries with you.

Your acknowledgement and recognition of their distress may be sufficient for some people, and they may be able to resolve their distress themselves if they know that they can obtain additional support from you if necessary.

Care workers need to give individuals the chance to decide whether they want to talk about the causes of distress

The effects of your interactions

You need to be aware of the ways in which you are using your own communication skills to interact with someone who is distressed. While you are taking into account the person's body language and the clues of non-verbal communication, you will need to be conscious of the messages your own non-verbal communication is sending. You need to demonstrate openness with an open welcoming position, but don't encroach on an individual's personal space as this often heightens tension. Make eye contact in a way that demonstrates you are willing to listen.

It is important you approach any individual who is distressed or displaying anger or excitement in a calm and non-threatening way. This will minimise the risks to the individual, to any other people in the immediate area and to yourself. If at any point you feel your personal safety is at risk you should immediately summon help.

Getting help

No one is able to deal with every situation with which they are faced, and you may feel that a particular situation is beyond your capability. This is nothing to be ashamed of. Knowing your own limitations is important and demonstrates a higher degree of maturity and self-awareness than taking risks. Contact other members of your team or other professionals with the experience to deal with the situation – never hesitate to summon help when you feel unsure in dealing with an individual in distress.

A distressed person can become aggressive in some circumstances. If you observe a person becoming aggressive and potentially violent, as in the case of someone changing from crying or expressing anger to shouting or throwing things, then you should immediately summon help. Information on coping with aggression can be found in Unit HSC 336.

Anger is not always directed at others; it can be turned inwards to be directed against individuals themselves. You may be faced with a distressed, hurt and angry individual who makes it clear that he or she intends to self-harm. In this case you have a responsibility to take immediate action to protect the individual. You must also advise the individuals that you will have to take these steps to protect them and attempt to stop them from harming themselves.

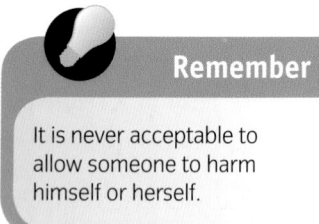

Remember

It is never acceptable to allow someone to harm himself or herself.

How to identify the support individuals need

When communicating with someone who is distressed, one of the first things to do is decide on the support and assistance you need to offer. People in distress can benefit from a wide range of different forms of support.

Deciding the level of support

Sometimes all people need is having their hand held to enable them to go on coping with the distress themselves. You should therefore always establish with the individual the extent of the help needed and what you can usefully provide. Providing unwanted support can sometimes be as damaging and as unhelpful as too little or none. The risks of providing unwanted support are:

- people may feel they are disempowered and are no longer able to help or support themselves – this is not good for their self-esteem or self-confidence
- people may feel you have interfered and they have been forced to reveal more about themselves and their personal life than they would have wished to
- people may become over-dependent on you for help and support and it may reduce their ability to manage for themselves.

The General Social Care Council (GSCC) code of practice for social care workers states that care workers must support service users' rights to control their lives and make informed choices about the services they receive (principle 1.3). Unwanted attention might breach this principle.

Offering too little or no help can have the following effects:

- people feel they are isolated and there is nobody who cares for them or is interested in their problems
- people may feel they are unworthy and not liked as individuals
- people may get very angry and frustrated at the apparent lack of care or interest from the rest of the world.

Not providing sufficient support may also breach the GSCC code.

The level of help and support you should offer is always best decided along with the individuals themselves. Wherever possible, this should be done through a process of discussion. Questions should be open-ended and clear, and designed to establish the correct level of support, such as 'I can see you're very upset – would it help to talk to me about it?' 'I can see you're very upset – would you like me to find you someone to talk to?'

There may be circumstances in which it is not possible to discuss this with individuals, perhaps because they are extremely agitated or angry or are in an exceedingly distressed state and unable to hold a calm conversation. It may even be that they are threatening to harm themselves or others. In these circumstances you will need to judge how best to intervene. You could try acting in the same way as you would when dealing with an individual who was calmer. For example, if you put your hand on the shoulder of someone who is sobbing and clearly very upset, the result could either be that the person shakes you off and walks away, or turns to you for a hug.

Attempts to comfort someone in distress may not always be welcome

Broadly, the necessary support you are likely to identify will probably fall into one of three categories, as shown in the table below.

Practical support	Giving information, offering a hug or hand holding, making a telephone call, providing transport or other practical assistance, contacting someone on behalf of the distressed person, or meeting an appropriate professional.
Emotional support	Using listening skills, using counselling skills.
Immediate emergency assistance	Summoning immediate help from a colleague, a senior member of staff, an appropriate professional, or the emergency services.

How to offer support

The types of support you might need to give are identified in the table above. You will need to ensure that you have access to sources of information and the appropriate resources that can be offered in particular circumstances. There are specialist organisations which will offer particular support for those who are bereaved, for those who are experiencing relationship difficulties or for those who are feeling depressed and may harm themselves. You should be sure that you can access all the relevant contact details.

Evidence indicator

Check the information stored in your workplace on sources of specialist support for people in distress, and the information on self-harming. If it is inadequate or out of date, create a plan of action for updating it. You might want to research it yourself and keep records for your portfolio.

Using communication skills

When you have identified the most appropriate support, you will need to use your communication skills to the full. If you have undertaken a training programme in counselling skills you will find this invaluable. This will not make you a counsellor, but it will provide you with the basic skills you need in your work setting to assist people on a day-to-day basis. A therapeutic treatment programme could then be offered through a qualified counsellor.

In a training programme for counselling skills you will learn how to begin to establish a supportive relationship by using skills such as setting boundaries, active listening, paraphrasing, mirroring and reflecting, challenging, facilitating, and ending a relationship. Such training can be extremely valuable and will enable you to offer a more comprehensive level of service.

Personal space is a very important issue in care work. A care worker who assumes it is acceptable to enter a service user's personal space without asking or explaining may be seen as being dominating or aggressive.

Face-to-face positions (orientation)

Standing or sitting face to face can send a message of being formal or being angry. A slight angle can create a more relaxed and friendly feeling.

Responding to others

How do you work out what another person might be feeling? Look at a person's facial expression. Much of what you will see will be in his or her eyes, but the eyebrows and mouth also tell you a lot about what someone is feeling.

Notice whether someone is looking at you, or at the floor, or at a point over your shoulder. Lack of eye contact should give a first indication that all may not be well. It may be that the individual is not feeling confident. He or she may be unhappy, or feel uneasy about talking to you. You will need to follow this up.

Look at how a person sits. Is he or she relaxed and comfortable, sitting well back in the chair, or tense and perched on the edge of the seat? Is he or she slumped in the chair with the head down? People who are feeling well and cheerful tend to hold their heads up, and sit in a relaxed and comfortable way. An individual who is tense and nervous, who feels unsure and worried, is likely to reflect that in the way he or she sits or stands. Observe hands and gestures carefully. Someone twisting his or her hands, or fiddling with hair or clothes, is signalling tension and worry. Frequent little shrugs of the shoulders or spreading of the hands may indicate a feeling of helplessness or hopelessness.

 CASE STUDY: Recognising body language

Mr Jarvis has just been admitted to a residential care home. He has severe arthritis and his mobility is very poor. He has some incontinence of urine. The arthritis in his hands, elbows and shoulders means that he is not able to carry out basic domestic tasks, but he can wash and dress, although he is slow and sometimes cannot manage the buttons.

He had been cared for at home by his wife until last week, when she suffered a massive stroke and died. Mr Jarvis has one son who lives 200 miles away. The son came at once when his mother died, and has stayed all week with his father. However, he now has to return to work and has arranged for his father to be admitted into residential care as a matter of urgency.

1 *What would you expect Mr Jarvis's facial expression to be?*

2 *Allowing for his physical difficulties, how do you think he would be sitting?*

3 *What do you think he would be doing with his hands?*

4 *What emotions and feelings is Mr Jarvis likely to be expressing through his body language?*

5 *How could Mr Jarvis's care worker support him to communicate?*

Giving out the signals

Being aware of your own body language is just as important as understanding the person you are talking to.

Keys to good practice: Communication skills

✓ Make sure that you maintain eye contact with the person you are talking to, although you should avoid staring! Looking away occasionally is normal, but if you find yourself looking around the room, or watching others, then you are failing to give people the attention they deserve.

✓ Be aware of what you are doing and try to think why you are losing attention.

✓ Sit where you can be comfortably seen. Don't sit where someone has to turn in order to look at you.

✓ Sit a comfortable distance away – not so far that any sense of closeness is lost, but not so close that you 'invade their space'.

✓ Make sure you are showing by your gestures that you are listening and interested in what people are saying – sitting half turned away gives the message that you are not fully committed to what is being said.

✓ Folded arms or crossed legs can indicate that you are 'closed' rather than 'open' to what someone is expressing.

✓ Nodding your head will indicate that you are receptive and interested – but be careful not to overdo it and look like a nodding dog!

✓ Lean towards someone to show that you are interested in what they are saying. You can use leaning forwards quite effectively at times when you want to emphasise your interest or support. Then move backwards a little at times when the content is a little lighter.

✓ Using touch to communicate your caring and concern is often useful and appropriate. Many individuals find it comforting to have their hand held or stroked, or to have an arm around their shoulders.

✓ Be aware of a person's body language, which should tell you if he or she finds touch acceptable.

✓ Always err on the side of caution if you are unsure about what is acceptable in another culture, for example with regard to touching.

Continued

- return promptly any e-mails you have received in error
- be careful not to give your password to anyone.

Active knowledge

Your organisation should have a policy for dealing with the filing and storing of e-mails about service users. Check this policy to ensure it is up to date with the latest data protection legislation. If necessary, arrange training sessions for your team members.

E-mail is a fast and efficient method of communication in most circumstances

Outgoing post

If you have to write information to send to another organisation, whether it is by letter or by fax or e-mail, you should be sure that the contents are clear, cannot be misunderstood and are to the point. Do not write a rambling, long letter which obliges recipients to hunt for the information they need.

It is likely that, within many organisations, you will need to show any faxes or letters to your supervisor or manager before they leave the premises. This safeguard is in place in many workplaces for the good reason that information being sent on behalf of your employer must be accurate and appropriate. As your employer is the person ultimately responsible for any information sent out, he or she will want to have procedures in place to check this.

Confidentiality

Confidentiality involves keeping information safe and only passing it on where there is a clear right to it and a clear need to do so. Confidentiality is an important right for all service users because:

- service users may not trust a care worker who does not keep information confidential

- service users may not feel valued or able to keep their self-esteem if their private details are shared with others
- service users' safety may be put at risk if details of their property and habits are shared publicly.

A professional service which maintains respect for individuals must keep private information confidential. There are legal requirements under the Data Protection Act 1998 to keep personal records confidential (see page 65).

Boundaries to confidentiality

Service users have a right to confidentiality, but also a responsibility in relation to the rights of others. Confidentiality often has to be kept within boundaries and the rights of others have to be balanced with the service user's rights. A care worker may have to tell his or her manager something learned in confidence. The information is not made public, so it is still partly confidential. Information may need to be passed to managers in the following situations.

Situation	Example of information that needs to be passed on
There is a significant risk of harm to a service user	An older person in the community refuses to put any heating on in winter; she may be at risk of harm from the cold.
A service user is in danger of being abused	A person explains that his son takes his money – he may be experiencing financial abuse.
There is a significant risk of harm to others	A person lives in a very dirty house with mice and rats, and may be creating a public health risk.
There is a risk to the care worker's health or well-being	A person is very aggressive, placing the care worker at risk.

Confidentiality and the need to know

Good care practice involves asking service users if we can let other people know things. It would be wrong to pass on even the date of a person's birthday without asking him or her first. Some people might not want others to celebrate their birthday – for example, Jehovah's Witnesses believe that it is wrong to do so. Whatever we know about a service user should be kept private unless the person tells us that it is acceptable to share the information. The exception to this rule is that information can be passed on when others have a right and a need to know it.

Some examples of people who have a need to know about work with service users are:

- managers – they may need to help make decisions which affect the service user

The purpose of keeping records

In any organisation records are kept for a variety of different purposes. The type of record that you keep is likely to be dictated by the purpose for which it is required. It could be:

- information that is needed for making decisions
- information to provide background knowledge and understanding for another worker
- information about family and contacts of people who are important to an individual
- information to be passed to another professional who is also involved in providing a caring service
- information to be passed from yourself to a colleague over a short space of time to ensure that the care you provide offers an element of continuity
- information to help in planning and developing services.

The kind of information that you may record to pass on within your own organisation may well be different from the types of record that you would keep if you were going to send that information to another agency, or if it was going into someone else's filing system.

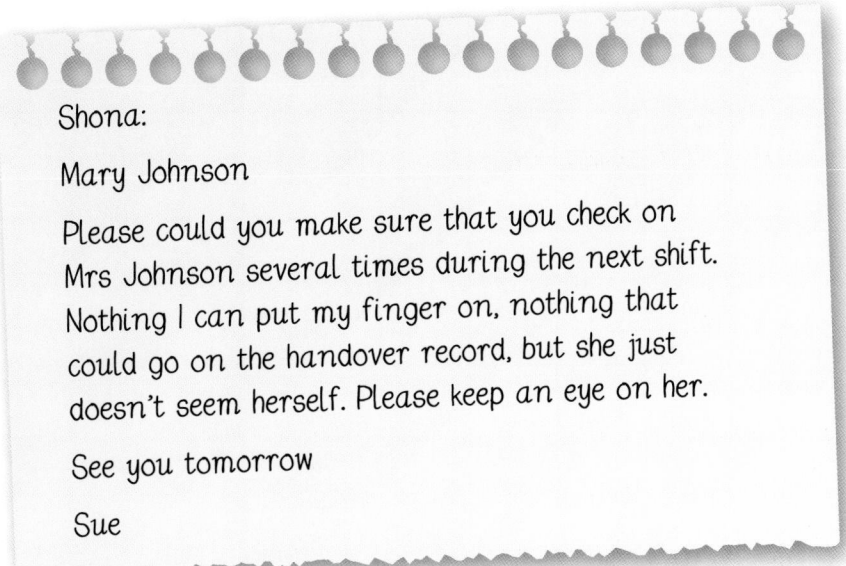

Shona:

Mary Johnson

Please could you make sure that you check on Mrs Johnson several times during the next shift. Nothing I can put my finger on, nothing that could go on the handover record, but she just doesn't seem herself. Please keep an eye on her.

See you tomorrow

Sue

An informal note like the one above is often used to pass on information which is not appropriate for a formal file or record sheet, but it is nevertheless important for a colleague to take note of. This is different from information which has to go outside the organisation – it would need to be formally written, and word processed using a more structured format.

Medical records

One of the very common means of transmitting information and keeping records in health and care is an observation chart recording temperature and blood pressure, like the one on the next page.

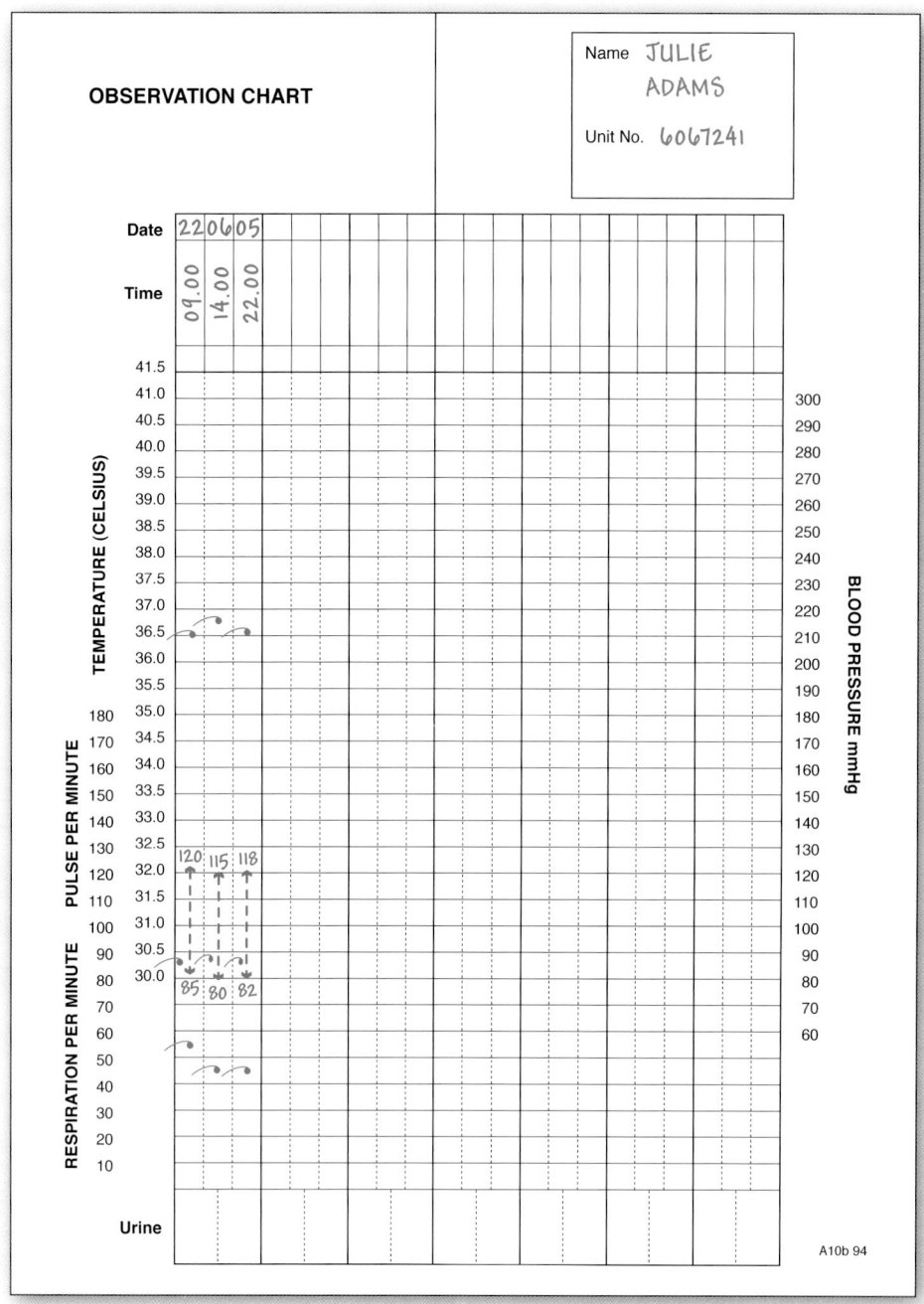

An observation chart

This is done in a very simple form on a graph, so it is easy to see at a glance if there are any problems. The purpose of this record is simply to monitor a person's physical condition so that everybody who is caring for him or her is able to check on the person's well-being.

If you were to put a written record into someone's case notes or to write a report for another agency or another professional, it is unlikely that you would include the actual charts. It is far more likely that you would include a comment or an interpretation of the information on the charts similar to the one on the next page.

Mrs J has shown no significant abnormalities in terms of raised temperature or blood pressure for the past week. It would seem to indicate her infection has now cleared up and her temperature has returned to normal after the very high levels of ten days ago.

Other types of record

Information which is likely to be used in making decisions about someone is very important. It may concern an older person who has been the subject of a protection conference, or someone with mental health problems where a background report is being provided to assist in decisions about how to best treat him or her.

Where such records are being kept for the purpose of assisting with decision making, it is important that reports are not written in such a way that people have to read through vast amounts of material before finding the key points. It may be necessary to include a significant amount of information in order to make sure that all of the background is there, but a summary at the beginning or the end is always useful for a reader in a hurry.

Why records are so important

If service user records are not managed in accordance with the Data Protection Act and Commission for Social Care Inspection regulations, service users might suffer a range of damaging consequences, including those shown below.

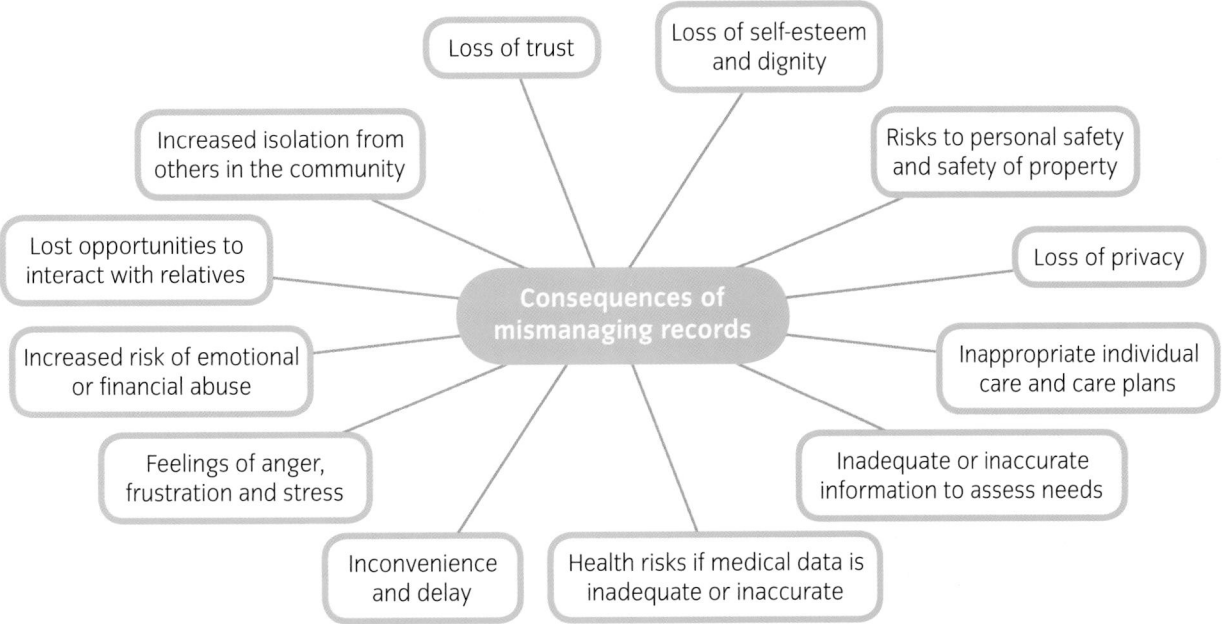

Loss of trust

Loss of self-esteem and dignity

Increased isolation from others in the community

Risks to personal safety and safety of property

Lost opportunities to interact with relatives

Loss of privacy

Consequences of mismanaging records

Increased risk of emotional or financial abuse

Inappropriate individual care and care plans

Feelings of anger, frustration and stress

Inadequate or inaccurate information to assess needs

Inconvenience and delay

Health risks if medical data is inadequate or inaccurate

How to record information

If you think about the purpose for which the information is to be used, this should help you to decide on the best way to record it. There would be little point in going to the trouble of typing out a piece of information that you were simply going to pass over to a colleague on the next shift. Alternatively, if you were writing something which was to go into someone's case notes or case file and be permanently recorded, then you would need to make sure that the information is likely to be of use to colleagues, or others who may need to have access to the file.

You may need to record and report:

- signs and symptoms indicating a change in the condition of an individual
- signs of a change in the care needs of an individual
- decisions you have made and actions you have taken relating to an individual's needs or condition
- difficulties or conflicts that have arisen, and actions taken to resolve them.

Active knowledge

Find out if your organisation has a policy about record-keeping and about where different types of information should be recorded and kept. Check whether there are clear guidelines on what should be handwritten and information that needs to be word processed.

You must make sure that you follow the guidelines and provide information in the format that your organisation needs. If you are unsure about how you should produce particular kinds of records, ask your manager.

Keys to good practice: Keeping records

There are certain golden rules which are likely to be included in any organisation's policy about keeping records and recording information:

✓ All information needs to be clear.

✓ It needs to be legible (particularly if you are handwriting it) – there is nothing more useless than a piece of information in a record file which cannot be read because someone's handwriting is poor.

✓ It should be to the point, not ramble or contain far more words than necessary.

✓ Any record should cover the important points clearly and logically.

Look at the following report on K by CS, K's key worker.

K has been bad this week. On Monday he wouldn't go to college. He said he felt ill but he didn't have a temperature or anything. I think he wanted to stay here and see his new girlfriend in the next lodge.

Tuesday 12 noon. After I had just fed him he vomited all over me. I know he can't help throwing up, but he could give me some warning so I didn't have to change all my clothes. I cleaned him up in the usual way.

Thursday we had archery in the lounge. K wanted to go in his wheelchair but he's supposed to use his sticks, so I told him he had to try with them. He got really stroppy and refused to go in the end. I think we ought to arrange some other activities for him that he can do in his own lodge. Then we won't have these fights about him getting about. What do you think?

1 *What is your opinion of this report? Consider the factual detail, the attitude shown towards K by his key worker, and the practical suggestions made.*

2 *List the improvements that you would make to this report.*

3 *What problems could be caused by poor report writing like this example?*

4 *If you were CS's manager, how would you respond to receiving a report like this?*

Methods of storing and retrieving records

Imagine going into a record shop which has thousands of CDs stored in racks but in no recognisable order; they are not filed by the name of the artist, nor by the title of the album. Imagine how much time it would take to trace the particular album that you are looking for. Anything from REM to the Rolling Stones to Mantovani would be all jumbled together! This is exactly what it is like with a filing system – unless there is a system that is easily recognisable and allows people to trace files quickly and accurately, it is impossible to use.

Records are stored in filing systems. These may be manual or computerised. All organisations will have a filing system, and one of the first jobs you must undertake is to learn how to use it.

Some organisations have people who deal specifically with filing, and they do not allow untrained people to access the files. This is likely to be the case if you work for a large organisation, such as an NHS trust. Smaller agencies are likely to have a general filing system to which everyone in the organisation has access. This is exactly the kind of situation where files and records are likely to go missing and to be misplaced.

If you learn to appreciate the importance of records and the different systems that can be used for their storage, then you can assist rather than hinder the process of keeping records up to date, in the right place and readily accessible when people need them.

Manual systems

In a manual filing system the types of file used can vary. The most usual type of file is a brown manila folder with a series of documents fastened inside. Other types include ring binders, lever arch files and bound copies of computer printouts.

All of the files have to be organised (indexed) and stored in a way which makes them easily accessible whenever they are required.

Alphabetical system

If there are not too many files, they can be kept in an alphabetical system in a simple filing cabinet or cupboard. In this sort of system, files are simply placed according to the surname of the person they are about. They are put in the same order as you would see names in a telephone directory, starting with A and working through to the end of the alphabet, with names beginning *Mc* being filed as *Mac* and *St* being filed as *Saint*. GPs' patient records are usually kept using an alphabetical system.

Numerical systems

Where there are large numbers of files an alphabetical system would not work. Imagine the numbers of M. Johnsons or P. Williamses who would appear as patients in a large hospital! In that situation an alphabetical filing system would become impossible to manage, so large organisations give their files numbers, and they are stored in number order. Clearly, a numerical system needs to have an index system so that a person's name can be attached to the appropriate number.

A hospital is likely to give a patient a number which will appear on all relevant documentation so that it is always possible to trace his or her medical notes. However, there still needs to be an overall record to attach that person's name and address to that particular set of case notes, and these days this is normally kept on a central computer.

Other indexing systems

It could be that, instead of files being organised alphabetically, they may be organised according to the different services an agency offers. For example, they could be kept under 'Mental health services', 'Care in the community services', 'Services for children' and so on. Within these categories files would be kept in alphabetical order. In a similar way, files may be organised under geographical areas.

Computerised systems

If your organisation uses a computerised system, there will be very clear procedures which must be followed by everyone who accesses the system. The procedures will vary depending on the system used, but usually involve accessing files through a special programme, which may well have been written either especially for your organisation, or specifically for record-keeping in health and care.

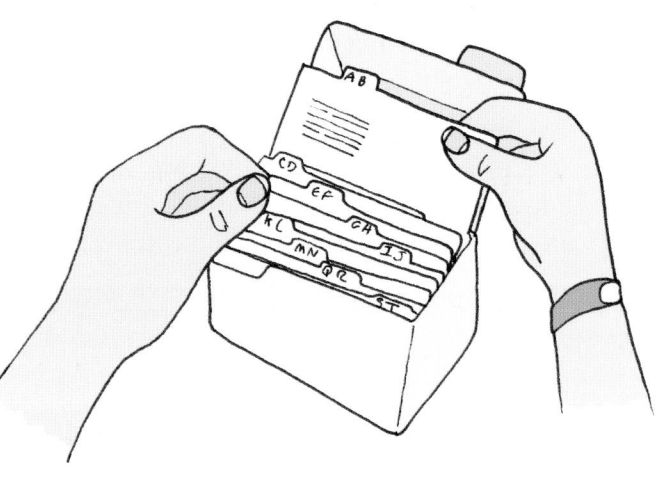

An alphabetical card index

You are unlikely to be able to delete or alter any information which is in someone's file on a computer. It is possible that you will only be able to add information in very specific places, or it could be that files are 'read only' and you cannot add any information to them. This process, because it will not allow people to change or alter files, does have the advantage that information is likely to remain in a clear format. It is less likely to become lost or damaged in the way that manual files are. After all, it is really not possible to leave a computer system on a bus!

With a computerised filing system, there will be clear procedures to be followed

A computerised system enables organisations to keep a great deal more information in much less space. Although they can be expensive to install and to set up, the advantages outweigh the disadvantages in the long run. It also means that everyone in the organisation has to learn how to operate the system and how to use the computer – this is a new skill for many people. It is, however, a skill worth learning if it enables you to record and use information more accurately and effectively.

Evidence indicator

Find out about the filing system used in your workplace. Check how much information is kept in files, and how much on computer. Find out if the system is alphabetical or numerical, and ask someone who understands it to show you how to use it. Make notes for your portfolio.

Other types of records

Most organisations maintain electronic records for accounts, suppliers, personnel and all essential business records. There will be a back-up for any electronically held information; this may be a paper system or off-site electronic back-up.

Useful information about advice and support services in the area could be maintained in a resource area or filing system, so that helpful leaflets and information packs are not left in a heap on a shelf or a window sill! An electronic index of useful websites, with links, can be very valuable for service users and their families if they have computer access and are comfortable accessing information in this way.

Remember

Filing systems can work extremely well if they are properly run. They work efficiently and effectively in most organisations as long as a few basic rules are followed by everyone who uses them (see the table below).

Some basic rules about filing

Do	Don't
Leave a note or card (or something similar) when you borrow a file from a manual filing system	Remove an index card from a system
Return files as soon as possible	Keep files lying around after you have finished with them
Enter information clearly and precisely	Alter or move around the contents of a file, or take out or replace documents which are part of someone's file
Be sure that you access electronic files strictly within your permitted level of access	Make any changes to files unless permitted to do so
Make sure you log in and out correctly	Copy any part of an electronic record system
	Forget to log out

There may also be occasions when access is restricted for other reasons; possibly because someone is seriously ill and there are medical reasons for limiting access, or because of a legal restriction such as a court order. In either case, it should be clearly recorded on the individual's record and your supervisor will advise you about the restrictions. If you are working in a supervisory capacity, it will be part of your role to ensure that junior staff are aware of these restrictions.

Abuse is dealt with in depth in Unit HSC 35 (page 200), but it can never be repeated often enough that individuals have a right to be protected from abuse, and you must report immediately any abuse you see or suspect.

Active knowledge

You need a colleague or friend to try this role play. One of you should be the person who has come to visit and the other the care worker who has to say that a friend or relative will not see him or her. Try using different scenarios – angry, upset, aggressive, and so on. Try at least three different scenarios each. By the time you have practised a few times, you may feel better equipped to deal with the situation when it happens in reality.

If you cannot find anyone to work with you, it is possible to do a similar exercise by imagining three or four different scenarios and then writing down the words you would say in each of the situations.

Security of property

Property and valuables belonging to individuals in care settings should be safeguarded. It is likely that your employer will have a property book in which records of all valuables and personal possessions are entered.

There may be particular policies within your organisation, but as a general rule you are likely to need to:

- make a record of all possessions on admission
- record valuable items separately
- describe items of jewellery by their colour, for example 'yellow metal' not 'gold'
- ensure that individuals sign for any valuables they are keeping, and that they understand that they are liable for their loss
- inform your manager if an individual is keeping valuables or a significant amount of money.

Evidence indicator

Find out where the property book is in your workplace, and how it is filled in. Check who has the responsibility to complete it. If you are likely to have to use the book at any time, make sure you know exactly what your role is. Do you have to enter the property in the book, then give it to someone else to deal with the valuables? Do you have to make sure the valuables are safe? Do you have to give the individual a copy of the entry in the book? Ask the questions in advance – don't leave it until you have to do it.

Make notes of your findings for your portfolio.

It is always difficult when items go missing in a care setting, particularly if they are valuable. It is important that you check all possibilities before calling the police.

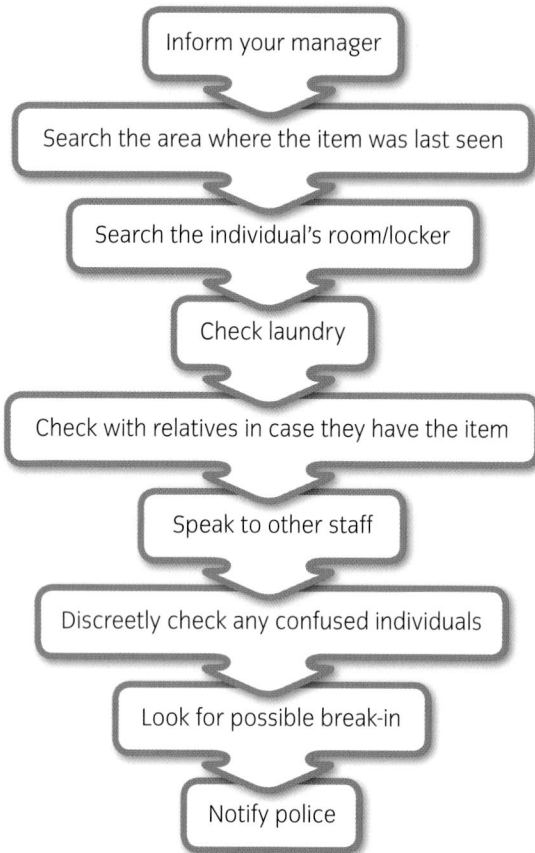

Inform your manager

Search the area where the item was last seen

Search the individual's room/locker

Check laundry

Check with relatives in case they have the item

Speak to other staff

Discreetly check any confused individuals

Look for possible break-in

Notify police

Action stages when property goes missing

Outside the usual care setting

There are always additional health and safety considerations when you are providing care or support to service users outside the care environment. For example, if you are planning a visit or holiday trip, you may need to consider the following:

- accessibility
- safety of premises and potential hazards
- accessibility and safety of transport
- provision of safe toilet facilities
- security of people, property and travel documents
- safety checks on any equipment
- instructions for using any unfamiliar equipment
- provision for special dietary arrangements
- insurance.

A change in environment can prove unsettling for some individuals, and extra vigilance may be needed to ensure that vulnerable people are not distressed by the changes.

The legal framework

The settings in which you provide care are generally covered by the Health and Safety at Work Act 1974 (HASAWA). This Act has been updated and supplemented by many sets of regulations and guidelines, which extend it, support it or explain it. The regulations most likely to affect your workplace are shown in the diagram below.

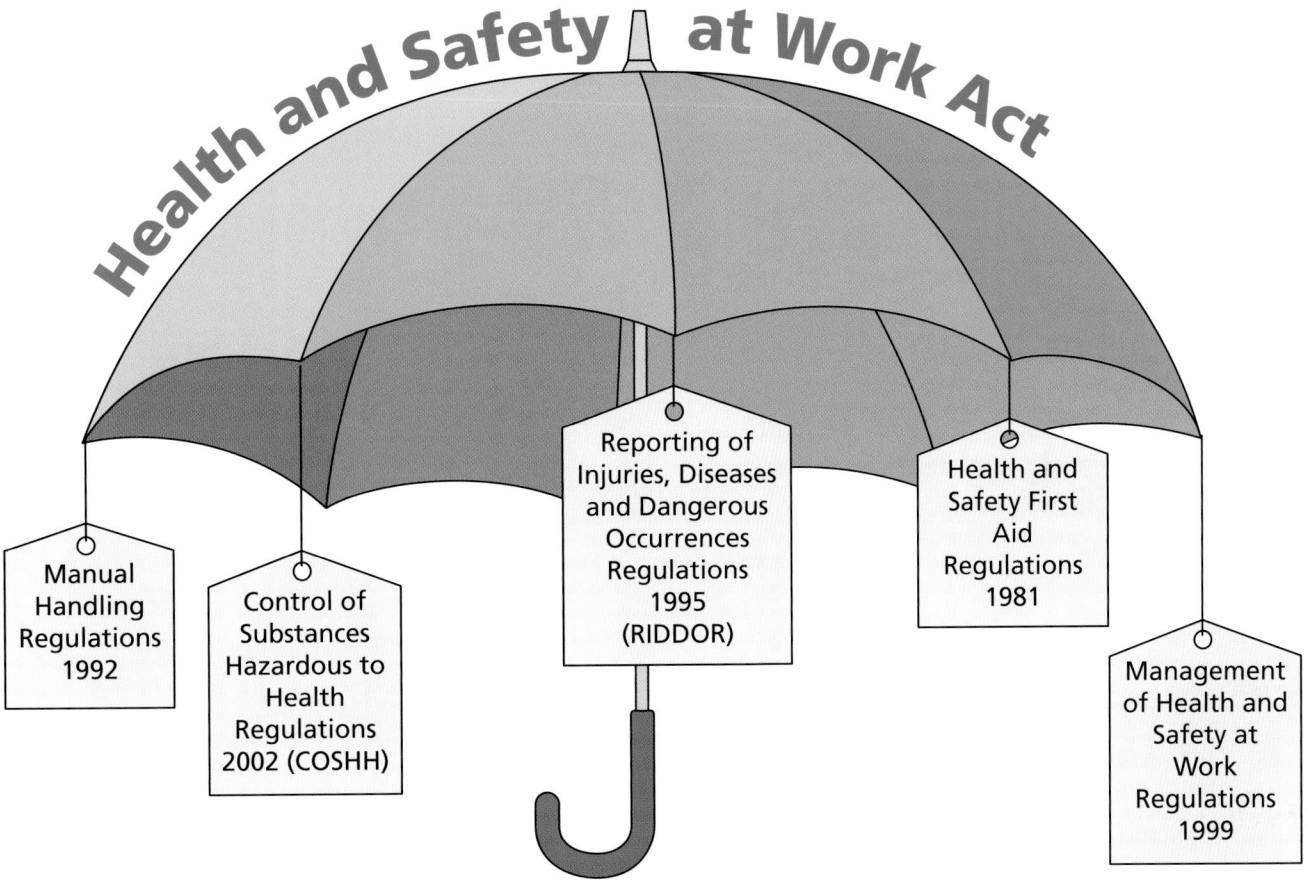

The Health and Safety at Work Act is like an umbrella

You and the law

There are many regulations, laws and guidelines dealing with health and safety. You do not need to know the detail, but you do need to know where your responsibilities begin and end.

The laws place certain responsibilities on both employers and employees. For example, it is up to the employer to provide a safe place in which to work, but the employee also has to show reasonable care for his or her own safety.

Employers have to:
- provide a safe workplace
- ensure that there is safe access to and from the workplace
- provide information on health and safety
- provide health and safety training
- undertake risk assessment for all hazards.

Workers must:

- take reasonable care for their own safety and that of others
- co-operate with the employer in respect of health and safety matters
- not intentionally damage any health and safety equipment or materials provided by the employer.

Both the employee and employer are jointly responsible for safeguarding the health and safety of anyone using the premises.

Each workplace where there are five or more workers must have a written statement of health and safety policy. The policy must include:

- a statement of intention to provide a safe workplace
- the name of the person responsible for implementing the policy
- the names of any other individuals responsible for particular health and safety hazards
- a list of identified health and safety hazards and the procedures to be followed in relation to them
- procedures for recording accidents at work
- details for evacuation of the premises.

Active knowledge

Find out where the health and safety policy is for your workplace and make sure you read it.

The Health and Safety Executive

Britain's Health and Safety Commission (HSC) and the Health and Safety Executive (HSE) are responsible for the regulation of almost all the risks to health and safety arising from work activity in Britain. The Health and Safety Commission is sponsored by the Department of Work and Pensions and is accountable to the Minister of State for Work.
The HSE's job is to help the Health and Safety Commission ensure that risks to people's health and safety from work activities are properly controlled.

The Health and Safety Executive (www.hse.gov.uk) states:

Our mission is to protect people's health and safety by ensuring risks in the changing workplace are properly controlled.

The HSC believes that prevention is better than cure, and two key roles are providing information and support to ensure that workplaces are safe and enforcement in order to ensure that legislation is adhered to. The HSE has the power to prosecute employers who fail in any way to safeguard the health and safety of people who use their premises.

Risk assessment

Risk assessment is designed for employers and self-employed people, who are required by law to identify and assess risks in the workplace. This includes any situations where potential harm may be caused. There are many regulations that require risks to be assessed and some are covered by European Community directives. These include:

- Management of Health and Safety at Work Regulations 1999
- Manual Handling Operations Regulations 1992 (amended 2002)
- Personal Protective Equipment at Work Regulations 1992
- Health and Safety (Display Screen Equipment) Regulations 1992 (amended 2002)
- Noise at Work Regulations 1989
- Control of Substances Hazardous to Health Regulations 2002 (COSHH)
- Control of Asbestos at Work Regulations 2002
- Control of Lead at Work Regulations 2002.

There are other regulations that deal with very specialised risks such as major hazards and ionising radiation. However, these are not considered to be common risks in most workplaces.

There are five key stages to undertaking a risk assessment, which involve answering the following questions.

- What is the purpose of the risk assessment?
- Who has to assess the risk?
- Whose risk should be assessed?
- What should be assessed?
- When should the risk be assessed?

The Management of Health and Safety at Work Regulations 1999 state that employers have to assess any risks which are associated with the workplace and work activities. This means all activities, from walking on wet floors to dealing with violence. Having carried out a risk assessment, the employer must then apply **risk control measures**. This means that actions must be taken to reduce the risks. For example, alarm buzzers may need to be installed or extra staff employed, as well as steps such as providing extra training for staff or written guidelines on how to deal with a particular hazard.

Key term

Risk control measures: Actions taken in order to reduce an identified risk.

Risk assessments are vitally important in order to protect the health and safety of both you and the service user. You should always check that a risk assessment has been carried out before you undertake any task, and then follow the steps identified in the assessment in order to reduce the risk.

However, do not forget that you must balance the individual wishes and preferences of each individual who uses your service with your own safety and the safety of others. Some examples of this principle are discussed in the section on manual handling on page 100.

Risks in someone's home

Of course, the situation is somewhat different if you work in an individual's own home. Your employer can still carry out risk assessments and put risk control measures in place, such as a procedure for working in twos in a situation where there is a risk of violence. What cannot be done is to remove environmental hazards such as trailing electrical flexes, rugs with curled up edges, worn patches on stair carpets or old equipment. All you can do is to advise the person whose home it is of the risks, and suggest how things could be improved. You also need to take care!

Control of Substances Hazardous to Health (COSHH)

What are hazardous substances? There are many substances hazardous to health – nicotine, many drugs, even too much alcohol! The COSHH Regulations apply to substances which have been identified as toxic, corrosive or irritant. This includes cleaning materials, pesticides, acids, disinfectants and bleaches, and naturally occurring substances such as blood, bacteria, etc. Workplaces may have other hazardous substances which are particular to the nature of the work carried out.

The Health and Safety Executive states that employers must take the following steps to protect employees from hazardous substances.

Step 1

Find out what hazardous substances are used in the workplace and the risks these substances pose to people's health.

Step 2

Decide what precautions are needed before any work starts with hazardous substances.

Step 3

Prevent people being exposed to hazardous substances, but where this is not reasonably practicable, control the exposure.

Step 4

Make sure control measures are used and maintained properly, and that safety procedures are followed.

Step 5

If required, monitor exposure of employees to hazardous substances.

Remember

- It may be your workplace, but it is the person's home. If you work in an individual's home or long-term residential setting, you have to balance the need for safety with the rights of people to have their living space the way they want it.

- Both you and the individuals using the service are entitled to expect a safe place in which to live and work, but remember their rights to choose how they want to live.

Step 6

Carry out health surveillance where assessment has shown that this is necessary, or COSHH makes specific requirements.

Step 7

If required, prepare plans and procedures to deal with accidents, incidents and emergencies.

Step 8

Make sure employees are properly informed, trained and supervised.

Every workplace must have a COSHH file, which should be easily accessible to all staff. This file lists all the hazardous substances used in the workplace. It should detail:

- where they are kept
- how they are labelled
- their effects
- the maximum amount of time it is safe to be exposed to them
- how to deal with an emergency involving one of them.

Remember

Hazardous substances are not just things like poisons and radioactive material – they are also substances such as cleaning fluids and bleach.

Active knowledge

You must ensure that you and all staff know the location of the COSHH file in your workplace. Read the contents of the file, especially information about the substances you use or come into contact with and what the maximum exposure limits are. You do not have to know the detail of each substance but the information you need should be contained in the COSHH file, which must be kept up to date.

If you have to work with hazardous substances, make sure that you take the precautions detailed in the COSHH file. This may be wearing gloves or protective goggles, or it may involve limiting the time you are exposed to the substance or only using it in certain circumstances.

The COSHH file should also give you information about how to store hazardous substances. This will involve using the correct containers as supplied by the manufacturers. All containers must have safety lids and caps, and must be correctly labelled.

Never use the container of one substance for storing another, and *never* change the labels.

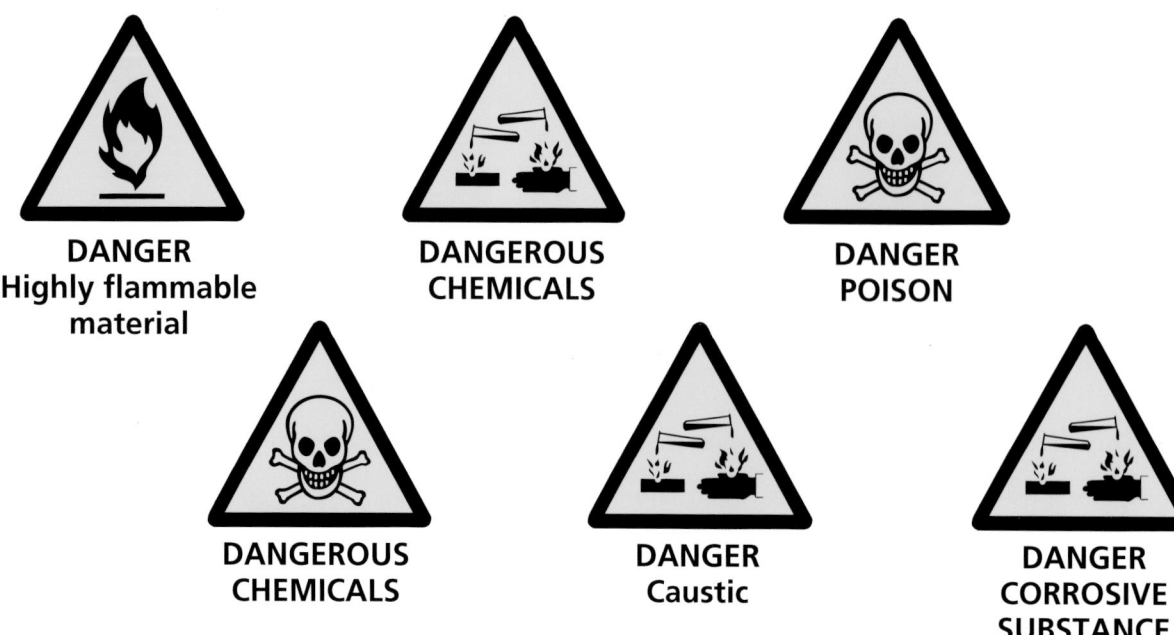

DANGER
Highly flammable
material

DANGEROUS
CHEMICALS

DANGER
POISON

DANGEROUS
CHEMICALS

DANGER
Caustic

DANGER
CORROSIVE
SUBSTANCE

These symbols, which warn you of hazardous substances, are always yellow

The symbols above indicate hazardous substances. They are there for your safety and for the safety of those you care for and work with. Before you use *any* substance, whether it is liquid, powder, spray, cream or aerosol, take the following simple steps:

- check the container for the hazard symbol
- if there is a hazard symbol, go to the COSHH file
- look up the precautions you need to take with the substance
- make sure you follow the procedures, which are intended to protect you.

If you are concerned about a substance being used in your workplace which is not in the COSHH file, or if you notice incorrect containers or labels being used, report this to your supervisor. Once you have informed your supervisor, it becomes his or her responsibility to act to correct the problem.

Reporting of Injuries, Diseases and Dangerous Occurrences (RIDDOR)

Reporting accidents and ill-health at work is a legal requirement. All accidents, diseases and dangerous occurrences should be reported to the Incident Contact Centre. The Centre was established on 1 April 2001 as a single point of contact for all incidents in the UK. The information is important because it means that risks and causes of accidents, incidents and diseases can be identified. All notifications are passed on to either the local authority Environmental Health department, or the Health and Safety Executive, as appropriate.

Your employer needs to report:

- deaths
- major injuries (see below)
- accidents resulting in more than three days off work
- diseases
- dangerous occurrences.

Reportable major injuries and diseases

Reportable injuries	Reportable diseases
fracture other than to fingers, thumbs or toes	certain poisonings
amputation	
dislocation of the shoulder, hip, knee or spine	some skin diseases such as occupational dermatitis, skin cancer, chrome ulcer, oil folliculitis acne
loss of sight (temporary or permanent)	
chemical or hot metal burn to the eye or any penetrating injury to the eye	lung diseases including occupational asthma, farmer's lung, pneumoconiosis, asbestosis, mesothelioma
injury resulting from an electric shock or electrical burn leading to unconsciousness or requiring resuscitation or admittance to hospital for more than 24 hours	
any other injury which leads to hypothermia (getting too cold), heat-induced illness, or unconsciousness; requires resuscitation; or requires admittance to hospital for more than 24 hours	infections such as leptospirosis, hepatitis, tuberculosis, anthrax, legionellosis (Legionnaires' disease) and tetanus
unconsciousness caused by asphyxia (suffocation) or exposure to a harmful substance or biological agent	
acute illness requiring medical treatment, or leading to loss of consciousness, arising from absorption of any substance by inhalation, ingestion or through the skin	other conditions such as occupational cancer, certain musculoskeletal disorders, decompression illness and hand-arm vibration syndrome
acute illness requiring medical treatment where there is reason to believe that this resulted from exposure to a biological agent or its toxins or infected material.	

Dangerous occurrences

If something happens which does not result in a reportable injury, but which clearly could have done, then it may be a dangerous occurrence which must be reported immediately.

Accidents at work

If accidents or injuries occur at work, either to you, other staff or to an individual you are caring for, then the details must be recorded. For example, someone may have a fall, or slip on a wet floor. You must record the incident regardless of whether there was an injury.

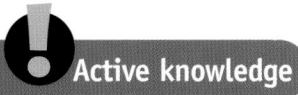

Active knowledge

Check that you understand fully all the terms used in the table above.

Your employer should have procedures in place for making a record of accidents, either an accident book or an accident report form. This is not only required by the RIDDOR regulations, but also, if you work in a residential or nursing home, by the Commission for Social Care Inspection.

Any accident book or report form must comply with the requirements of the Data Protection Act 1998 by making sure that the personal details of those involved cannot be read by others using the book. This can be ensured by recording personal details on a tear-off part of the form so that only an anonymous description of the accident is left, or by using individual, numbered and recorded forms that are then logged at a central point. However it is done, it is a legal requirement that people's personal details are not available for others to see unless consent has been given.

Make sure you know where the accident report forms or the accident book are kept, and who is responsible for recording accidents. It is likely to be your manager. An example of an accident report form is given in the Appendix, on page 382.

You must report any accident in which you are involved, or which you have witnessed, to your manager or supervisor. It may be useful to make notes, as in the example below, as soon as possible after the incident so that details on the accident report form can be complete and accurate.

Date: 24.8.05   **Time:** 14.30 **hrs**   **Location:** Main lounge

Description of accident:

PH got out of her chair and began to walk across the lounge with the aid of her stick. She turned her head to continue the conversation she had been having with GK, and as she turned back again she appeared not to have noticed that MP's handbag had been left on the floor. PH tripped over the handbag and fell heavily, banging her head on a footstool.

She was very shaken and although she said that she was not hurt, there was a large bump on her head. P appeared pale and shaky. I asked J to fetch a blanket and to call Mrs J, deputy officer in charge. Covered P with a blanket. Mrs J arrived immediately. Dr was sent for after P was examined by Mrs J.

Dr arrived after about 20 mins and said that she was bruised and shaken, but did not seem to have any injuries.

She wanted to go and lie down. She was helped to bed.

Incident was witnessed by six residents who were in the lounge at the time: GK, MP, IL, MC, CR and BQ.

Signed: **Name:**

An example of notes for the completion of an accident report form

Any medical treatment or assessment which is necessary should be arranged without delay. If an individual has been involved in an accident, you should check if there is anyone he or she would like to be contacted, perhaps a relative or friend. If the accident is serious, and you cannot consult the individual – because he or she is unconscious, for example – the next of kin should be informed as soon as possible.

Complete a report, and ensure that all witnesses to the accident also complete reports. You should include the following in any accident report (see the example on the previous page):

- date, time and place of accident
- person/people involved – bearing in mind the Data Protection Act
- circumstances and details of exactly what you saw
- anything that was said by the individuals involved
- the condition of the individual after the accident
- steps taken to summon help, time of summoning help and time when help arrived
- names of any other people who witnessed the accident
- any equipment involved in the accident.

Evidence indicator

Look at the incident/accident report form for your workplace. Does the form provide enough information? The purpose of the form is to provide sufficient information to:

- ensure the individual receives the proper medical attention
- provide information for treatment at a later date, in case of delayed reactions
- give information to any inspector who may need to see the records
- identify any gaps or need for improvements in safety procedures
- provide information about the circumstances in case of any future legal action.

Think about how you would re-design the report form if necessary, and what further headings you would include. Use the list above as a checklist to make sure you have covered everything you need.

Make sure that the accident form complies with the requirements of the Data Protection Act 1998. Keep your notes as evidence for your portfolio.

Dealing with hazardous waste

As part of providing a safe working environment, employers have to put procedures in place to deal with waste materials and spillages. There are various types of waste, which must be dealt with in particular ways. The types of hazardous waste you are most likely to come across are shown in the table on the next page, alongside a list of the ways in which each is usually dealt with. Waste can be a source of infection, so it is very important that you follow the procedures your employer has put in place to deal with it safely.

Type of waste	Method of disposal
Clinical waste – used dressings	Yellow bags, clearly labelled with contents and location. This waste is incinerated.
Needles, syringes, cannulas ('sharps')	Yellow sharps box. Never put sharps into anything other than a hard plastic box. This is sealed and incinerated.
Body fluids and waste – urine, vomit, blood, sputum, faeces	Cleared and flushed down sluice drain. Area to be cleaned and disinfected.
Soiled linen	Red bags, direct into laundry; bags disintergrate in wash. If handled, gloves must be worn.
Recyclable instruments and equipment	Blue bags, to be returned to the Central Sterilisation Services Department (CSSD) for recycling and sterilising.

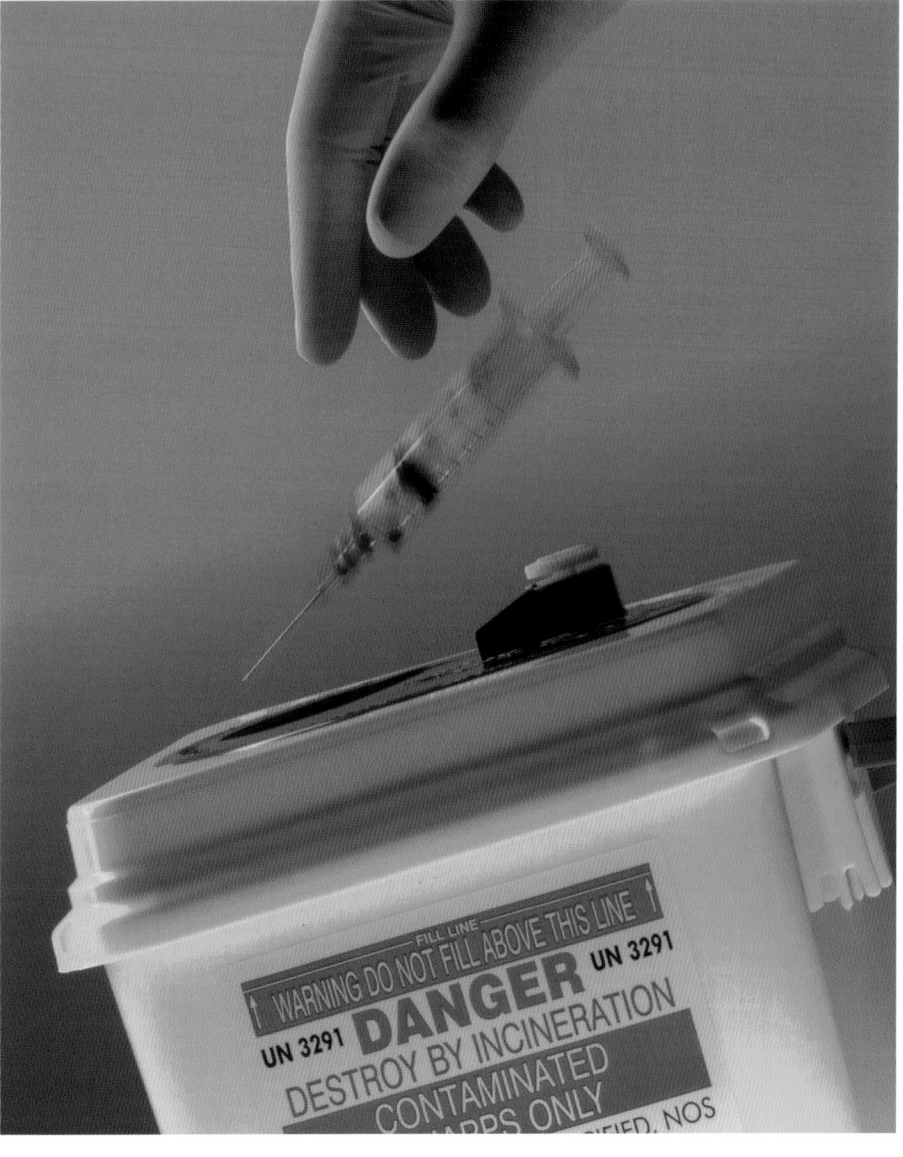

Needles and syringes should be put into a hard plastic box, which is sealed and incinerated

Remember

- Other people will have to deal with the waste after you have placed it in the bags or containers.

- Make sure it is properly labelled and in the correct containers.

The Manual Handling Operations Regulations 1992 require employers to avoid all manual handling where there is a risk of injury 'so far as it is reasonably practical'. Everyone from the European Commission to the Royal College of Nursing has issued policies and directives about avoiding lifting. Make sure you check out the policies in use in your workplace and that you understand them.

Lifting Operations and Lifting Equipment Regulations (1992) (LOLER)

These regulations came into effect on 5 December 1998 and apply to all workplaces. An employee does not have any responsibilities under LOLER but under the Management of Health and Safety at Work Regulations, employees have a duty to ensure that they take reasonable care of themselves and others who may be affected by the actions that they undertake.

Employers do have duties under LOLER. They must ensure that all equipment provided for use at work is:

- sufficiently strong and stable for the particular use and marked to indicate safe working loads
- positioned and installed to minimise any risks
- used safely – that is the work is planned, organised and performed by competent people
- subject to ongoing thorough examination and, where appropriate, inspection by competent people.

In addition employers must ensure:

- lifting operations are planned, supervised and carried out in a safe way by competent people
- equipment for lifting people is safe
- lifting equipment and accessories are thoroughly examined
- a report is submitted by a competent person following a thorough examination or inspection.

Lifting equipment designed for lifting and moving loads must be inspected at least annually, but any equipment that is designed for lifting and handling people must be inspected at least every six months. A nominated competent person may draw up an examination scheme for this purpose.

If employees provide their own lifting equipment, this is covered by the regulations.

Manual lifting

There is almost no situation in which manual lifting and handling could be considered acceptable, but the views and rights of the individual being lifted must be taken into account and a balance achieved.

Remember

- Always use lifting and handling aids.
- There is no such thing as a safe lift.
- Use the aids which your employer is obliged to provide.

On the rare occasions when it is still absolutely necessary for manual lifting to be done, the employer has to make a 'risk assessment' and put procedures in place to reduce the risk of injury to the employee. This could involve ensuring that sufficient staff are available to lift or handle someone safely, which can often mean that four people are needed.

Remember

- Your employer has a statutory duty to install lifting equipment, but it is your responsibility to use the equipment that is provided.

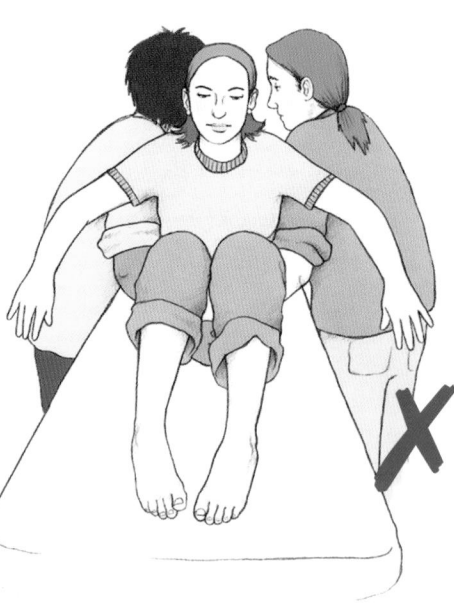

Use the aids which your employer is obliged to provide

CASE STUDY: Using safe lifting procedures

Kirsty is a new care assistant at a day centre for adults with disabilities. She was trained to use a hoist as part of a moving and handling course in her previous job. Although there is a mobile hoist at the day centre, Kirsty has noticed that none of the staff use it. On several occasions she has seen individuals being manually lifted from their wheelchairs by the staff, working in pairs.

One morning a service user, Valerie, asked Kirsty to accompany her to the toilet. Kirsty knew that Valerie would need to be helped from her chair onto the toilet, so she went to get the hoist. As she passed the other staff one of them said: 'Oh, you don't want to bother with that thing. Val isn't very heavy – it's much easier to just lift her yourself. Anyway, I don't think the hoist works any more.'

1 *What should Kirsty do next?*

2 *If the hoist does not work, what should Kirsty do?*

3 *What could be the consequences of lifting incorrectly:*

  a *to the staff*

  b *to the individuals they are attempting to lift?*

4 *What training and safety procedures would you recommend for this day centre?*

5 *Are you confident that your own moving and handling skills are up to date? If not, what steps are you taking to improve them?*

Your employer should arrange for all staff to attend a moving and handling course. You must attend one each year, so that you are up to date with the safest possible practices.

If you do have to lift, what should you do?

Encourage all individuals to help themselves – you would be surprised how much 'learned helplessness' exists. This can occur when care workers find it is quicker and easier to do things themselves rather than allowing a person to do it for himself or herself. If service users accept that someone else will take over all care, they may stop making the effort to maintain their independence – in short, they learn how to become helpless.

It is also essential that the views of the person being moved are taken into account. While you and your employer need to make sure that you and other staff are not put at risk by moving or lifting, it is also important that the person needing assistance is not caused pain, distress or humiliation. Groups representing disabled people have pointed out that blanket policies excluding any lifting may infringe the human rights of an individual needing mobility assistance. For example, individuals may in effect be confined to bed unnecessarily and against their will by a lack of lifting assistance. A High Court judgement (A & B vs East Sussex County Council, 2003) found in favour of two disabled women who had been denied access to lifting because the local authority had a 'blanket ban' on lifting regardless of circumstances. Such a ban was deemed unlawful. It is likely that similar cases will be brought under the Human Rights Act 1998, which gives people protection against humiliating or degrading treatment.

The Disability Discrimination Act 1995 came fully into force in October 2004. It was introduced in several stages to take account of the time needed to meet its requirements. This included allowing time for service providers to consider making reasonable changes to their premises so that they could be accessed by disabled users.

Since October 1999, service providers have had to consider making reasonable adjustments to the way they deliver their services so that disabled people can use them. The new duties will apply to service providers where physical features make access to their services impossible or unreasonably difficult for disabled people.

How to contribute to infection control

The very nature of work in a care setting means that great care must be taken to control the spread of infection. You will come into contact with a number of people during your working day – an ideal opportunity for infection to spread. Infection which spreads from one person to another is called 'cross-infection'. If you work in the community, cross-infection is difficult to control. However, if you work in a residential or hospital setting, infection control is essential. There are various steps which you can take in terms of the way you carry out your work (wherever you work) which can help to prevent the spread of infection.

You do not know what viruses or bacteria may be present in any individual, so it is important that you take precautions when dealing with everyone. The precautions are called 'standard precautions' precisely because you need to take them with everyone you deal with. You must ensure that all staff are familiar with standard precautions and adhere to them.

Wear gloves

When	Any occasion when you will have contact with body fluids (including body waste, blood, mucus, sputum, sweat or vomit), or when you have any contact with anyone with a rash, pressure sore, wound, bleeding or any broken skin. You must also wear gloves when you clear up spills of blood or body fluids or have to deal with soiled linen or dressings.
Why	Because gloves act as a protective barrier against infection.

How

1 Check gloves before putting them on. Never use gloves with holes or tears. Check that they are not cracked or faded.

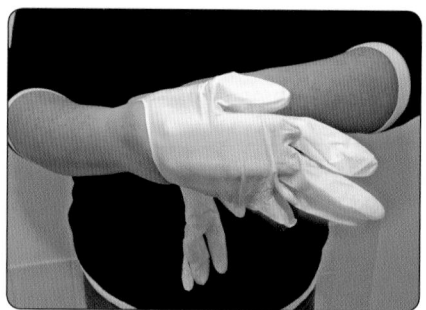

2 Pull gloves on, making sure that they fit properly. If you are wearing a gown, pull them over the cuffs.

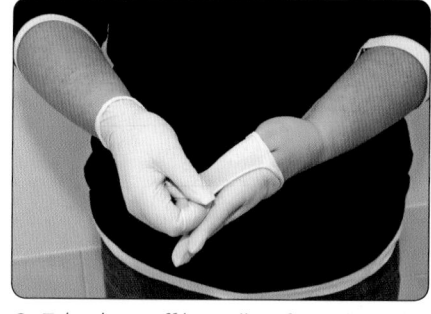

3 Take them off by pulling from the cuff – this turns the glove inside out.

4 Pull off the second glove while still holding the first so that the two gloves are folded together inside out.

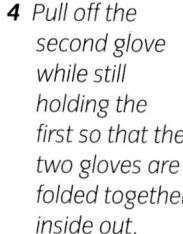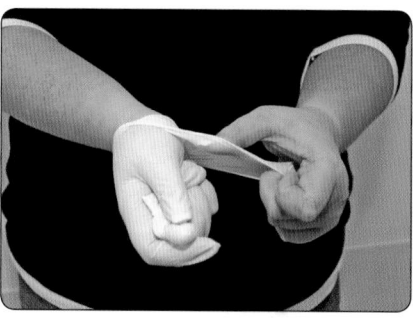

5 Dispose of them in the correct waste disposal container and wash your hands.

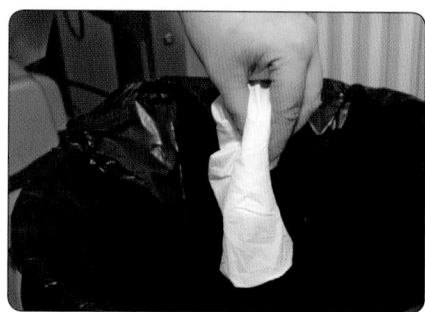

Symptoms

- Acute pain around the site of the injury
- Swelling and discoloration around the affected area
- Limbs or joints may be in odd positions
- Broken bones may protrude through the skin

Action for fractures

1   The important thing is to support the affected part. Help the casualty to find the most comfortable position.

2   Support the injured limb in that position with as much padding as necessary – towels, cushions or clothing will do.

3   Take the person to hospital or call an ambulance.

Do not:

- try to bandage or splint the injury
- allow the casualty to have anything to eat or drink.

Support the injured limb

Burns and scalds

There are several different types of burn; the most usual are burns caused by heat or flame. Scalds are caused by hot liquids. People can also be burned by chemicals or by electrical currents.

Symptoms

- Depending on the type and severity of the burn, skin may be red, swollen and tender, blistered and raw or charred
- Usually severe pain and possibly shock

Aims

- To obtain immediate medical assistance if the burn is over a large area (as big as the casualty's hand or more) or is deep
- To send for an ambulance if the burn is severe or extensive. If the burn or scald is over a smaller area, the casualty could be transported to hospital by car
- To stop the burning and reduce pain
- To minimise the possibility of infection

Action for burns and scalds

1   For major burns, summon immediate medical assistance.

2   Cool down the burn. Keep it flooded with cold water for 10 minutes. If it is a chemical burn, this needs to be done for 20 minutes. Ensure that the contaminated water used to cool a chemical burn is disposed of safely.

Cool the burn with water

3   Remove any jewellery, watches or clothing which are not sticking to the burn.

4   Cover the burn if possible, unless it is a facial burn, with a sterile or at least clean non-adhesive dressing. If this is not possible, leave the burn uncovered. For a burn on a hand or foot, a clean plastic bag will protect it from infection until it can be treated by an expert.

If clothing is on fire, remember the basics: *stop*, *drop*, *wrap* and *roll* the person on the ground.

Do not:

- remove anything which is stuck to a burn
- touch a burn, or use any ointment or cream
- cover facial burns – keep pouring water on until help arrives.

Poisoning

People can be poisoned by many substances, drugs, plants, chemicals, fumes or alcohol.

Symptoms

Symptoms will vary depending on the poison.
- The person could be unconscious
- There may be acute abdominal pain
- There may be blistering of the mouth and lips

Aims

- To remove the casualty to a safe area if he/she is at risk, and it is safe for you to move him/her
- To summon medical assistance as a matter of urgency
- To gather any information which will identify the poison
- To maintain a clear airway and breathing until help arrives

Action for poisoning

1   If the casualty is unconscious, place him/her in the recovery position to ensure that the airway is clear, and that he/she cannot choke on any vomit.

2   Dial 999 for an ambulance.

3   Try to find out what the poison is and how much has been taken. This information could be vital in saving a life.

4   If a conscious casualty has burned mouth or lips, he or she can be given small frequent sips of water or cold milk.

Do not **try to make the casualty vomit.**

Remember

If a person's clothing is on fire, STOP – DROP – WRAP – ROLL:

- *Stop* him or her from running around.

- Get him/her to *drop* to the ground – push him/her if you have to and can do so safely.

- *Wrap* him/her in something to smother the flames – a blanket or coat, anything to hand. This is better if it is soaked in water.

- *Roll* him/her on the ground to put out the flames.

Electrical injuries

Electrocution occurs when an electrical current passes though the body.

Symptoms

Electrocution can cause cardiac arrest and burns where the electrical current entered and left the body.

Aims

- To remove the casualty from the current when you can safely do so
- To obtain medical assistance as a matter of urgency
- To maintain a clear airway and breathing until help arrives
- To treat any burns

Action for electrical injuries

There are different procedures to follow depending on whether the injury has been caused by a high or low voltage current.

Injury caused by high voltage current

This type of injury may be caused by overhead power cables or rail lines, for example.

1 Contact the emergency services immediately.

2 *Do not* touch the person until all electricity has been cut off.

3 If the person is unconscious, clear the airway.

4 Treat any other injuries present, such as burns.

5 Place in the recovery position until help arrives.

Injury caused by low voltage current

This type of injury may be caused by electric kettles, computers, drills, lawnmowers, etc.

1 Break the contact with the current by switching off the electricity, at the mains if possible.

2 It is vital to break the contact as soon as possible, but if you touch a person who is 'live' (still in contact with the current) you too will be injured. If you are unable to switch off the electricity, then you must

stand on something dry which can insulate you, such as a telephone directory, rubber mat or a pile of newspapers, and then move the casualty away from the current as described below.

3   Do not use anything made of metal, or anything wet, to move the casualty from the current. Try to move him/her with a wooden pole or broom-handle, even a chair.

4   Alternatively, drag him/her with a rope or cord or, as a last resort, pull by holding any of the person's dry clothing which is *not* in contact with his/her body.

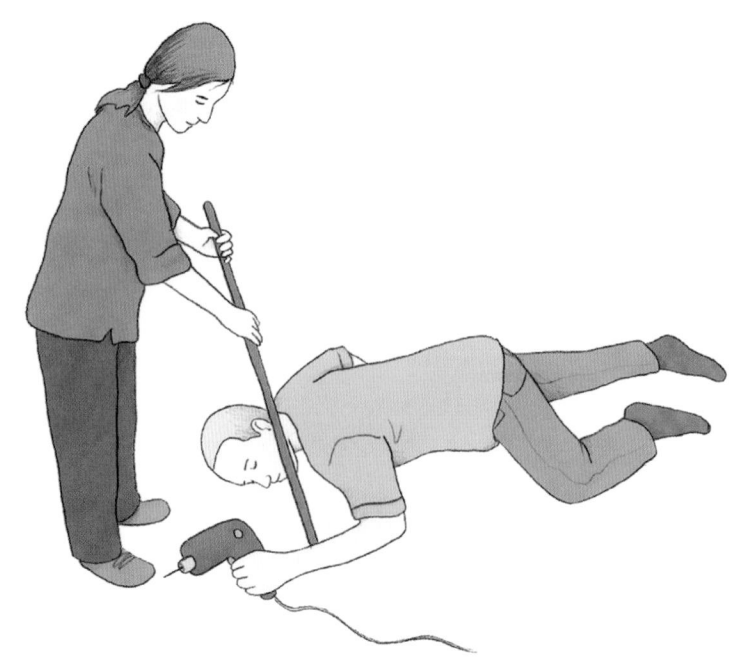

Move the casualty away from the current

5   Once the person is no longer in contact with the current, you should follow the same steps as with a high voltage injury.

Other ways to help

Summon assistance

In the majority of cases this will mean telephoning 999 and requesting an ambulance. It will depend on the setting in which you work and clearly is not required if you work in a hospital! But it may mean calling for a colleague with medical qualifications, who will then be able to make an assessment of the need for further assistance. Similarly, if you work in the residential sector, there should be a medically qualified colleague available. If you are the first on the scene at an emergency in the community, you may need to summon an ambulance for urgent assistance.

If you need to call an ambulance, try to keep calm and give clearly all the details you are asked for. Do not attempt to give information until it is asked for – this wastes time. Emergency service operators are trained to find out the necessary information, so let them ask the questions, then answer calmly and clearly.

Follow the action steps outlined in the previous section while you are waiting for help to arrive.

Assist the person dealing with the emergency

A second pair of hands is invaluable when dealing with an emergency. If you are assisting someone with first aid or medical expertise, follow all his or her instructions, even if you don't understand why. An emergency situation is not the time for a discussion or debate – that can happen later. You may be needed to help to move a casualty, or to fetch water, blankets or dressings, or to reassure and comfort the casualty during treatment.

Make the area safe

An accident or injury may have occurred in an unsafe area – and it was probably for precisely that reason that the accident occurred there! Sometimes, it may be that the accident has made the area unsafe for others. For example, if someone has tripped over an electric flex, there may be exposed wires or a damaged electric socket. Alternatively, a fall against a window or glass door may have left shards of broken glass in the area, or there may be blood or other body fluids on the floor. You may need to make the area safe by turning off the power, clearing broken glass or dealing with a spillage.

It may be necessary to redirect people away from the area of the accident in order to avoid further casualties.

Maintain the privacy of the casualty

You may need to act to provide some privacy for the casualty by asking onlookers to move away or stand back. If you can erect a temporary screen with coats or blankets, this may help to offer some privacy. It may not matter to the casualty at the time, but he or she has a right to privacy if possible.

Make accurate reports

You may be responsible for making a report on an emergency situation you have witnessed, or for filling in records later. Concentrate on the most important aspects of the incident and record the actions of yourself and others in an accurate, legible and complete manner.

 CASE STUDY: Dealing with a health emergency

On the way to lunch one Tuesday, Miss Shaw, who sometimes experiences incontinence, had a little 'accident' in the main hallway. Another resident coming along behind called out, 'Oh look! She's done a puddle!' and stopped to stare. Miss Shaw, feeling embarrassed and distressed, turned quickly to go back to her room and slipped on the wet floor, falling heavily on her hip. The first staff member on the scene was Maria.

1 *List the actions that Maria should take, in order.*

2 *Could this accident have been prevented? If so, how?*

3 *What follow-up actions or discussions would you recommend to the management?*

How to deal with witnesses' distress – and your own

People who have witnessed accidents can often be very distressed by what they have seen. The distress may be as a result of the nature of the injury, or the blood loss. It could be because the casualty is a friend or relative or simply because seeing accidents or injuries is traumatic. Some people can become upset because they feel helpless and do not know how to assist, or they may have been afraid and then feel guilty later.

You will need to reassure people about the casualty and the fact that he or she is being cared for appropriately. However, do not give false reassurance about things you may not be sure of.

You may need to allow individuals to talk about what they saw. One of the commonest effects of witnessing a trauma is that people need to repeat over and over again what they saw.

What about you?

You may feel very distressed by the experience you have gone through. You may find that you need to talk about what has happened, and that you need to look again at the role you played. You may feel that you could have done more, or you may feel angry with yourself for not having a greater knowledge about what to do.

There is a whole range of emotions which you may experience; Unit HSC 35 covers in detail the different emotions that may arise in similarly difficult circumstances involving abuse, and describes ways to cope with such feelings (page 217). You should be able to discuss them with your supervisor and use any support provided by your employer.

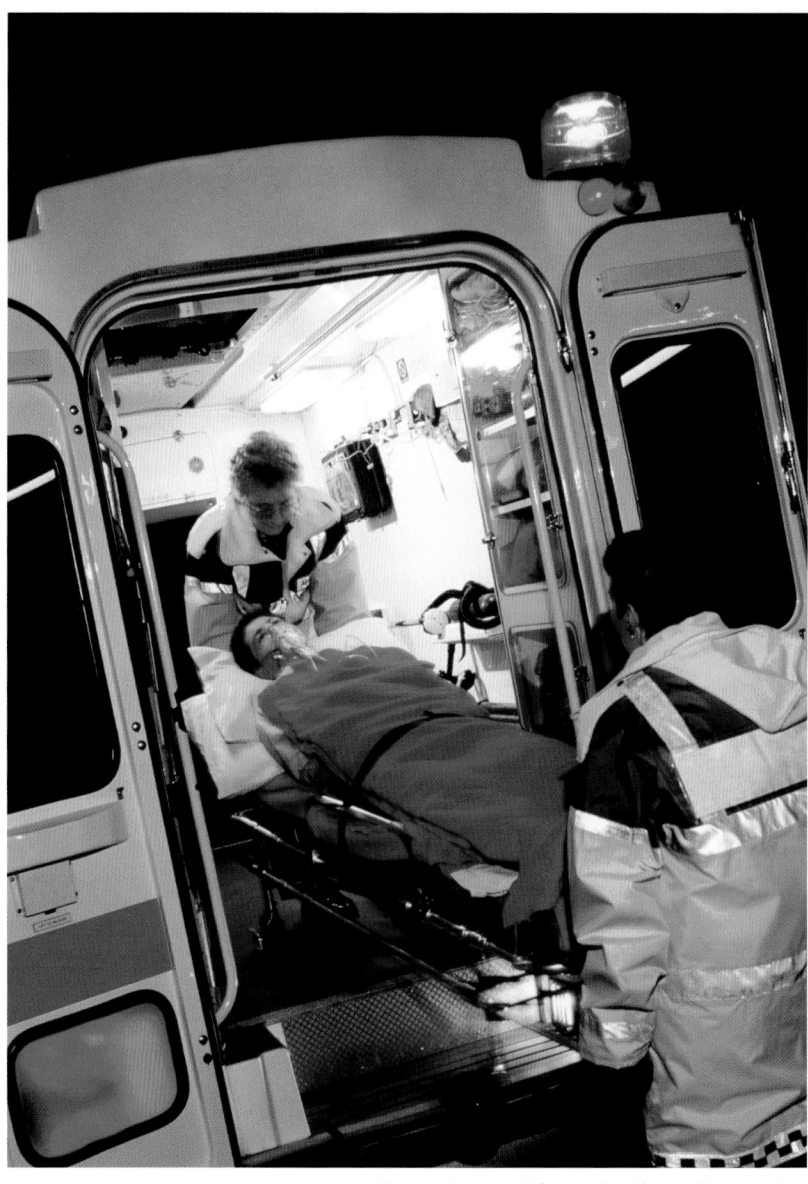

Witnessing accidents is often distressing

If you have followed the basic guidelines in this element, you will have done as much as could be expected of anyone at the scene of an emergency who is not a trained first aider.

Test yourself

1 In which conditions would it be safe for you to attempt to tackle a fire?

2 In what situations should you attempt first aid?

3 What is the single most important thing for an untrained person to do in a health emergency?

4 List three tasks you can carry out at the scene of a health emergency which do not necessarily involve first aid.

5 How would you talk to a casualty while you waited for help?

6 How would you support others who had witnessed an incident or accident?

HSC 32 UNIT TEST

1 What kind of substances would you expect to see in the COSHH file in your workplace?

2 Which tasks would you expect to find in the risk assessment file?

3 Is any specialised equipment in use in your workplace? If so, what sort of equipment? What basic precautions would you expect to follow when using it?

4 Describe your workplace rules on the way staff dress. What are the reasons for these rules?

5 What health and safety training would you expect staff in your workplace to undertake?

6 List at least three security precautions taken in your workplace.

Reflect on and develop your practice

The knowledge and skills addressed in this unit are the key to working effectively in all aspects of your practice. In order to work effectively, it is essential to know how to evaluate your work, how you can improve on what you do, and understand the factors which have influenced your attitudes and beliefs.

The care sector is constantly benefiting from new research, new developments, policies and guidelines. In order to offer the best possible level of service to those you care for, you need to make sure that you are up to date in work practices and knowledge, and aware of current thinking. As a worker in a care setting, you have a responsibility to constantly review and improve your practice. It is the right of service users to expect the best possible quality of care from those who provide it, and high quality care requires all practitioners to regularly reflect on their own practice and look at ways of improving.

Each organisation and each individual owes a **duty of care** to service users; this means that it is your responsibility to make sure that the service provided is the best it can possibly be. This is not an option, but a duty which you accept when you choose to become a professional care worker. The information in this unit will help you to identify the best ways to develop and update your own knowledge and skills.

What you need to learn

- How to explore your own values, interests and beliefs
- How your values, interests and beliefs influence your practice
- Reflective practice
- Support networks
- Learning from work practice
- Making good use of training/development opportunities
- Developing your own personal effectiveness
- Understanding new information
- How to ensure your practice is current and up to date
- Preparing a development plan.

Age	People may be classified as being children, teenagers, young adults, middle aged or old. Discrimination can creep into our thinking if we see some age groups as being 'the best', or if we make assumptions about the abilities of different age groups.
Gender	In the past, men often had more rights and were seen as more important than women. Assumptions about gender such as what is women's work and what is men's work can still result in mistakes and discrimination.
Race	People understand themselves in terms of ethnic categories such as being black or white, as European, African or Asian. Many people have specific national identities such as Polish, Nigerian, English or Welsh. Assumptions about racial characteristics and beliefs, or thinking that some groups are superior to others, result in discrimination.
Class	People differ in their upbringing, the kind of work they do and the money they earn. People also differ in the lifestyle they lead and the views and values that go with different levels of income and spending habits. People may discriminate against others because their class or lifestyle is different.
Religion	People grow up in different traditions of religion. For some people, spiritual beliefs are at the centre of their understanding of life. For others, religion influences the cultural traditions that they celebrate; for example, many Europeans celebrate Christmas even though they might not see themselves as practising Christians. Discrimination can take place when people assume that their customs or beliefs should apply to everyone else.
Sexuality	Many people see their sexual orientation as very important to understanding who they are. Gay and lesbian relationships are often discriminated against. Heterosexual people sometimes judge other relationships as 'wrong' or abnormal.
Ability	People may make assumptions about what is 'normal'. People with physical disabilities or learning difficulties may become labelled, stereotyped and discriminated against as damaged versions of 'normal' people.
Relationships	People choose many different lifestyles and emotional commitments, such as marriage, having children, living in a large family, living a single lifestyle but having sexual partners, or being single and not being sexually active. People live within different family and friendship groups. Discrimination can happen if people start to judge that one lifestyle is 'right' or best.
Politics	People can develop different views as to how a government should act, how welfare provision should be organised and so on. Disagreement and debate are necessary; but it is important not to judge people as bad or stupid because their views are different from ours.

Problems arise because our own culture and life experience may lead us to make assumptions as to what is right or normal. When we meet people who are different it can be easy to see them as 'not right' or 'not normal'. Different people see the world in different ways. Look at the illustration on the next page. Which is the 'normal' front of the cube?

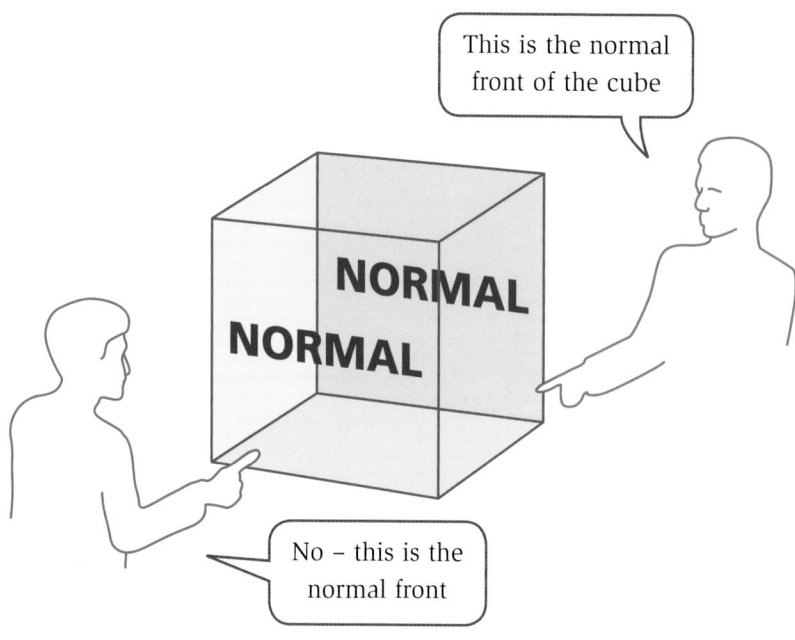

Which is the 'normal' front of the cube?

If a person was used to seeing this cube in one way, he or she might be sure that view was the right one. In the same way, our culture may lead us to think that some habits are more 'normal' than others, but in a multicultural, multifaith society such as the UK it is more difficult to define what 'normal' is.

Active knowledge

Take a piece of paper and draw a horizontal line, marking off each year of your life from the age of five so far. Then draw a vertical line at the left to create a scale of how happy your life has been. Try to reflect on your memories of the past, and draw a graph of your levels of happiness. What made particular years happy or unhappy for you? As you think back over your life, try to recall the people and the situations that affected you. Many of your beliefs and values have probably come about because of your interaction with these key people.

Try to imagine how you might have been different if you had lived in a different family or in a different community. Can you imagine how different life experiences create different belief systems? Can you see why it is vitally important not to make assumptions about what is right and wrong in different people's lives?

How your values, interests and beliefs influence your practice

Once you have begun to identify the major factors that have influenced your development, the next stage is to look at how they have affected the way in which you work and relate both to service users and colleagues. This is the basis of developing into a 'reflective practitioner' – someone who evaluates what he or she does.

Working in care requires that in order to be effective and to provide the best possible service for those you care for, you need to be able to think about and evaluate what you do and the way you work, and to identify your strengths and weaknesses. It is important that you learn to think about your own practice in a constructive way. Reflection and evaluation should not undermine your confidence in your own work; rather you should use them in a constructive way to identify areas that require improvement.

The ability to do this is an indication of excellent practice. Any workers in care who believe that they have no need to improve their practice or to develop and add to their skills and understanding are not demonstrating good and competent practice, but rather an arrogant and potentially dangerous lack of understanding of the nature of work in the care sector.

Becoming a thoughtful practitioner is not about torturing yourself with self-doubts and examining your weaknesses until you reach the point where your self-confidence is at zero! But it is important that you examine the work you have done and identify areas where you know you need to carry out additional development. A useful tool in learning to become a reflective practitioner is to develop a checklist which you can use, either after you have dealt with a difficult situation or at the end of each shift or day's work, to look at your own performance.

Checklist to evaluate practice

1 How did I approach my work?

2 Was my approach positive?

3 How did the way I worked affect the service users?

4 How did the way I worked affect my colleagues?

5 Did I give my work 100 per cent?

6 Which was the best aspect of the work I did?

7 Which was the worst aspect of the work I did?

8 Was this work the best I could do?

9 Are there any areas in which I could improve?

10 What are they, and how will I tackle them?

Reflective practice

The purpose of reflective practice is to improve and develop your practice by thinking about what you are doing. What is reflection and what does a worker need to be able to do in order to be able to improve his or her own practice? Reflection involves thinking things over; you could visualise reflection as reflecting ideas inside the mind like light bouncing between mirrors. Reflection involves complex mental processing that discovers new ideas or new inter-relationships between ideas. Reflection helps us to realise new ideas and make new sense of practice issues.

Imagine that every morning a resident who lives in a supported housing complex comes to the office to complain. The complaints might be about anything: sinks that don't drain quickly enough, cars parked too close to a wall, light bulbs that need changing (even though they still work!). Naturally this behaviour is annoying for the people who work in the office. But why does this resident complain?

Reflecting on the situation might enable a professional care worker to come up with some answers. But reflection can involve different levels of thinking. The most basic kind of reflection is simply to remember something. Different ideas that could develop from reflection are listed below.

Reflecting can help you to understand feelings and the wider issues involved

Just noticing what happens

Perhaps the interaction with this resident always follows a pattern. The person will wait for a short period and then launch into a verbal outburst about what is wrong. During this outburst the resident is unresponsive to the reactions of others. Having completed the outburst, the resident will look for a reaction and then storm off.

Just noticing this detail might provide a start to the reflective process. It would be so easy to label the resident as 'difficult' or 'challenging', and then use this label as if it were an explanation – and no further thinking were required. Just noticing the detail of what happens may help us to avoid labelling.

Reflection in order to make sense of a situation

What does the resident's pattern of behaviour mean? Perhaps this confrontational exchange represents a release of tension. Perhaps the resident does not have the social and emotional skills to engage in more sociable conversations. Perhaps the resident is trying to create a sense of belonging within the housing complex, and confrontation is chosen as the method because of limited social skills.

Reflection may not give us the correct answer, but trying to make sense of a situation helps us to be open to new ideas.

Going deeper – trying to understand feelings

What does the resident feel like when he or she comes to complain? Like so many people, the resident may feel a little isolated – a little insecure. Perhaps, like so many people, this resident is thinking 'If I don't feel good, then someone else is to blame'. Perhaps these emotions become focused on trivia such as light bulbs.

Thinking about feelings might help to generate extra ideas about what could be happening.

Going deeper – reflecting on wider issues

A care worker thinking about the problems that service users experience might reflect on the significance of these feelings. There are people who always search for other people to blame whenever anything is perceived to be less than perfect. But maybe we all tend to do this! Maybe we feel that 'they' should do something about climate change, about house prices, or about holes in the road. Perhaps we all like to retreat into a childlike state, expecting a kind parent to make the world comfortable and perfect for us.

Reflection that takes a wide view can involve new thoughts that could, for example, help us to understand ourselves better. Perhaps the difference between the resident's behaviour in the example above and our own behaviour is that we are more skilled at knowing how, when and where it is safe to 'have a moan'.

Reflection that results in new ways of thinking

How far do we take responsibility for our own emotions? If you were a person who had assumed that your emotions were all caused by outside events, it could be a major shock to find that your own thinking can directly influence your feelings. Many of the assumptions we make about life are hard to change. Abandoning the belief that someone else should make my life better and deciding that I am responsible for my life could represent a huge shift in thinking.

Remember

The purpose of reflection is to improve and develop your own practice.

Reflection on our own assumptions is not something that can happen on a daily basis. This kind of reflection involves an extreme shift in thinking that could change people's lives.

How deeply does your own reflective thinking go? As long as you reflect enough to get beyond the labelling stage, you are on the right path. The important thing is to think positively about areas of your work that you can improve. Reflection that does not identify areas for improvement is of little value – in fact, it can be highly destructive.

CASE STUDY: Seeking constructive feedback

Lewis works in a large residential setting for elderly adults where one of the people he cares for is Mrs Kaur, an Indian woman who speaks very little English. Mrs Kaur has many relatives who visit her regularly, and has long and animated conversations with them. But when she has no visitors, Mrs Kaur is very quiet. She hardly responds at all when Lewis tries to talk to her and is unwilling to talk to the other residents or to take part in any of the activities on offer. Lewis is concerned that Mrs Kaur may feel isolated; he would like to be able to communicate with her better and to improve his own practice.

1 *What are the barriers to communication between Lewis and Mrs Kaur?*

2 *Who could Lewis speak to about the situation?*

3 *What other actions could he take to improve his practice?*

Learning

When you have identified skills you would like to improve, the next step is to set about learning them. One of the best-known theories about the way in which people learn is the Lewin/Kolb cycle of experiential learning.

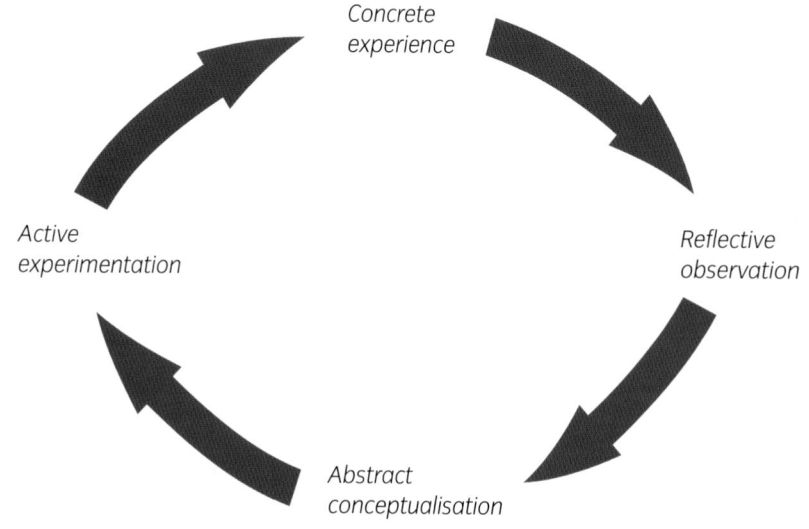

Kolb's cycle

Basically, this cycle means the following.

- Something happens to you or you do something; it can be an unusual event or something you do every day (**concrete experience**).
- You think about it (**reflective observation**).
- You work out some general rules about it, or you realise that it fits into a theory or pattern you already know about (**abstract conceptualisation**).
- Next time the same situation occurs, you apply your rules or theories (**active experimentation**).
- This will make your experience different from the first time, so you will have different factors to think about and different things to learn – so the cycle continues. You never stop learning.

Imagine that you are working with a man who has a learning difficulty. It is the first time you have met him and you are offering him a drink at lunchtime. You offer a glass of orange squash by placing it in front of him. He immediately pushes the glass away with a facial expression that you take to express disgust.

Within Kolb's learning cycle you have had a concrete experience.

Stage 1

Stage 1 of the learning cycle is the experience that this service user has rejected your offer of orange squash. But why has he reacted in this way?

Stage 2

Stage 2 involves thinking through some possible reasons for the reaction. Perhaps he doesn't like orange squash? Perhaps he doesn't like the way you put it in front of him? Perhaps he doesn't like to take a drink with his meal? Could it be an issue to do with social group membership? For example, could a cold drink symbolise childhood status for this individual? Does he see adult status as defined by having a hot drink? Reflection on the non-verbal behaviour of the service user may provide a range of starting points for interpreting his actions.

Stage 3

Kolb's third stage involves trying to make sense of our reflections. What do we know about different cultural interpretations of non-verbal behaviour? What are the chances that the way we placed the drink in front of the person has been construed as an attempt to control or dominate him? We didn't intend to send this message, but the service user may have interpreted our behaviour on an emotional level as being unpleasant. The more we know about human psychology and social group membership the more we can analyse the service user's reaction. We need to choose the most likely explanation for the service user's behaviour using everything we know about people.

Stage 4

Kolb's fourth stage involves 'experimenting', or checking out ideas and assumptions that we may have made. The worker might attempt to modify his or her non-verbal behaviour to look supportive. The worker might show the service user a cup and saucer to indicate the question: 'Is this what you would like'? If the service user responds with a positive non-verbal response, the worker would have been around the four stages of the cycle and would have solved the problem in a way that valued the individuality and diversity of the individual.

Workers might expect to have to go round this 'learning cycle' a number of times before they were able to correctly understand and interpret a service user's needs.

How quickly can you work through these four stages? Would you be able to think through these issues while working with the service user, or would you need to go away and reflect on practice? The answer to this question might depend on the amount of experience you have had in similar situations.

What is your learning style?

Honey and Mumford (1982) developed a theory based on this idea of a four-stage process of learning from experience. They theorised that some people develop a preference for a particular part of the learning cycle. Some people enjoy the activity of meeting new people and having new experiences, but these 'activists' may not get so much pleasure from reflecting, theorising and finding answers to individual needs. Some people mainly enjoy sitting down and thinking things through. These are 'reflectors'. Some people enjoy analysing issues in terms of established theoretical principles; these people are 'theorists'. Finally, some people prefer trying out new ideas in practice – these people are 'pragmatists'.

Active knowledge

Think about the ways in which *you* learn new things. Do you tend to use one part of the learning cycle more than others? Think about ways in which you could develop your skills in other parts of the cycle.

Honey and Mumford have argued that the ideal way to approach practical learning is to balance all the components of the learning cycle. Some people can achieve this more holistic approach. For other people it might be important to recognise their own biases and to try to compensate for an over-reliance on one style.

Honey and Mumford's theory of learning styles fits the four-stage learning cycle as follows:

How to use training and development

You should work with your supervisor to prepare for any training you receive, and to review it afterwards. You may want to prepare for a training session by:

- reading any materials which have been provided in advance
- talking to your supervisor or a colleague who has attended similar training, about what to expect
- thinking about what you want to achieve as a result of attending the training.

Keys to good practice: Training

Make the most of training by:

✓ preparing well

✓ taking a full part in the training and asking questions about anything you don't understand

✓ collecting any handouts and keeping your own notes of the training.

Think about how to apply what you have learned to your work by discussing the training with your supervisor later. Review the ways in which you have benefited from the training.

Evidence indicator

Think about the last training or development session you took part in and write a short report.

- Describe the preparations you made beforehand so that you could benefit fully from it.
- Describe what you did at the session; for example, what and how did you contribute, and what did you learn? Do you have a certificate to show that you participated in the session? Do you have a set of notes?
- How did you follow up the session? Did you review the goals you had set yourself, or discuss the session with your supervisor?
- Describe how you have used what you learned at the session. For example, how has the way you work changed, and how have your service users and colleagues benefited from your learning?

Developing your own personal effectiveness

The health and social care sector is one which constantly changes and moves on. New standards reflect the changes in the profession, such as the emphasis on quality services, the focus on tackling exclusion, and the influence of the culture of rights and responsibilities. There has been a huge increase in understanding in all parts of the sector, and a recognition of the satisfaction that comes from working alongside service users as partners and directors of their own care, rather than as passive receivers of services.

Developments in technology have brought huge strides towards independence for many service users, thus promoting a changing relationship with care workers; at the same time, technological developments have brought different approaches to the way in which work in care is carried out and the administration and recording of service provision.

Legislation and the resulting guidelines are a feature of the work of the sector. Sadly, many of the new guidelines, policies and procedures result from enquiries and investigations which followed tragedies, errors and neglect.

Despite all this, much of what we do in the care sector will remain the same; the basic principles of caring, treating people with dignity and respect, ensuring they have choice and promoting independence will continue, and the skills of good communication remain as vital as ever.

Being aware of new developments

There are many ways in which you can ensure that you keep up to date with new developments in the field of care, and particularly those which affect your own area of work. You should not assume that your workplace will automatically inform you about new developments, changes and updates which affect your work – you must be prepared to actively maintain your own knowledge base and to ensure that your practice is in line with current thinking and new theories. The best way to do this is to incorporate an awareness of the need to constantly update your knowledge into all of your work activities. If you restrict your awareness of new developments to specific times, such as a monthly visit to the library, or a training course every six months, you are likely to miss out on a lot of information.

CASE STUDY: Researching sleep deprivation

Beth, a senior care assistant, has recently started to work nights on a rota system. Unfortunately, at first things didn't go as well as she had hoped. Everyone said she would get used to it, but that simply didn't happen. At 3 o'clock in the morning, no matter how busy she was, she found herself getting light-headed and feeling quite nauseous. The other major problem was that she found sleeping during the day quite difficult. She managed to get through her first week, but dreaded the next time it was her turn on nights. She felt that the quality of her care would be unsafe if she didn't learn to cope.

Beth mentioned her concerns to Paul, a nursing friend. It turned out that he had once researched sleep deprivation, and found that there are all sorts of ways of coping. He recommended that she look at one or two helpful websites, and also that she read some of the research on night working – she could use both the local trust library and her own local library. The websites he suggested were: www.sleepeducation.com and www.bbc.co.uk/science/humanbody/sleep.

Beth looked at the websites and the research, found them very helpful and followed some of the advice she received. She is now able to cope better and more safely with her night shifts.

1 *Was Beth right to be concerned and to follow up her concerns, or should she just have tried to get used to it?*

2 *Look at these websites, or find similar ones on sleep yourself. Can you identify three strategies that Beth could adopt to make her night working and daytime sleeping more effective?*

3 *How could she communicate what she finds out to her colleagues?*

Sources of information

The media

The area of health and care is always in the news, so it is relatively easy to find out information about new studies and research. You will need to pay attention when watching television and listening to radio news bulletins to find out about new developments, legislation, guidelines and reports related to health and care service users and workers.

Active knowledge

For one week keep a record of every item which relates to health and care services which you hear on a radio bulletin, see in a television programme, or read in a newspaper article. You are likely to be surprised at the very large number of references you manage to find.

Articles in newspapers and professional journals are excellent sources of information. When reporting on a recently completed study, they usually give information about where to obtain a copy of it.

Reports and reviews

You can read the findings of enquiries into the failures experienced within social work, health and social care, and this might provide you with a focus for reflection. In the past there have been many cases where children and adults have been neglected or abused and social services have failed to protect vulnerable people adequately. Currently there is great national concern about the cleanliness and safety of hospital wards. While you may not be involved in policy-making decisions with respect to these services, there may be many principles such as 'whistle blowing' that are relevant in your own work setting. Many past serious failings might have been preventable if people had been able to identify the issues and take action earlier.

As well as reflecting on failures of the service, it will be important to reflect on positive practice. The Commission for Social Care Inspection (CSCI) includes brief anecdotes that help to explain the positive role of standards and inspection in improving the quality of life for service users, in some of its documents designed for the public. The CSCI website at www.csci.org.uk might provide you with one starting point for exploring ideas on successful approaches to care practice.

Conferences

Professional journals also carry advertisements for conferences and training opportunities. You may also find such information in your workplace. There is often a cost involved in attending these events, so the restrictions of the training budget in your workplace may mean that you cannot attend.

However, it may be possible for one person to attend and pass on the information gained to others in the workplace, or to obtain conference papers and handouts without attending.

The Internet

The development of information technology, and in particular the Internet, has provided a vast resource of information, views and research.

There are clearly some limitations to using the Internet; for example, many people are reluctant to look for information through that route because they are not confident about using computers. However, the use of computers in the health and care sector is becoming increasingly widespread and important. If you have access to a computer, using the Internet is a simple process that you could easily learn.

The Internet provides a vast amount of information

Another disadvantage is that you need to be wary of the information you obtain on the Internet, unless it is from accredited sources such as a government department, a reputable university or college, or an established research centre. Make every effort to check the validity of what you are reading. The World Wide Web provides free access to vast amounts of information, but it is an unregulated environment – anyone can publish information on the Internet, and there is no requirement for it to be checked or approved. People can publish their own views and opinions, which may not be based on fact. These views and opinions from a wide range of people are valuable and interesting in themselves, but be careful that you do not assume anything to be factually correct unless it is from a reliable source.

Treated with care, the Internet can prove to be one of the speediest and most useful tools in obtaining up-to-date information.

Your supervisor and colleagues

Never overlook the obvious: one of the sources of information which may be most useful to you is close at hand – your own workplace supervisor and colleagues. They may have many years of experience and accumulated knowledge which they will be happy to share with you. They may also be updating their own practice and ideas, and may have information that they would be willing to share.

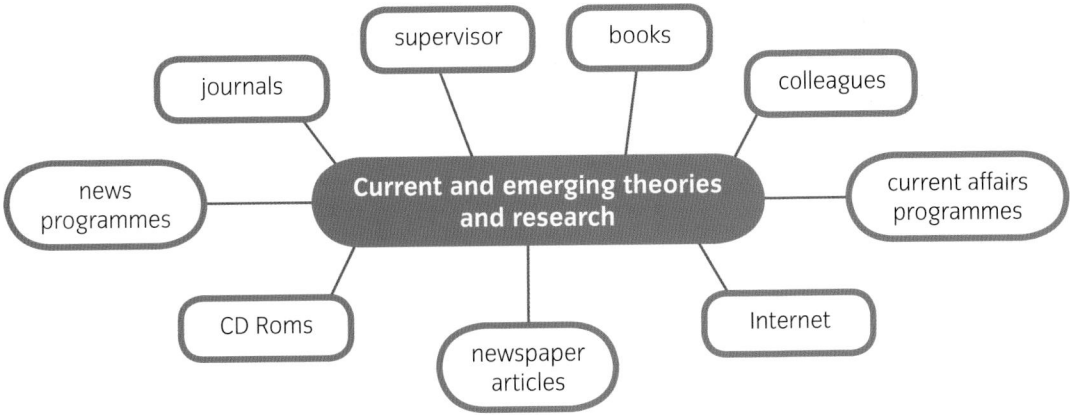

Information can be found from a wide range of sources

Understanding new information

Reading and hearing about new studies and pieces of research is all very well, but you must understand what it is that you are reading. It is important that you know how new theories are developed and how research is carried out.

Reliability and validity

There are specific methods of carrying out research to ensure the results are both reliable and valid. Research is judged on both of these factors, and you need to be able to satisfy yourself that the reports you read are based on reliable and valid research.

Reliability means the results would be repeated if someone else were to carry out the same piece of research in exactly the same way. **Validity** means that the conclusions that have been drawn from the research are consistent with the results, consistent with the way in which the research was carried out and consistent in the way in which the information has been interpreted.

The research process

You will need to understand some of the basic terms which are used when discussing research in any field.

- **Primary research** refers to information or data which is obtained directly from the research carried out, not from books or previously published work.
- **Secondary research** refers to information obtained from books, previously published research and reports, CD Roms, the Internet, etc. – any information obtained from work carried out by others. For example, if you were asked to write an assignment you are most likely to find the information from secondary sources such as textbooks or the Internet, rather than carry out a research project yourself in order to establish the information you need.

The information obtained from research is often referred to as **data**. It is called data regardless of whether it is in numbers or in words.

There are two broad areas of approach to research and they determine both the way in which the research is carried out and the type of results that are obtained. The first is referred to as **quantitative**, the second is **qualitative**.

Quantitative research

This approach has developed from the way in which scientists carry out laboratory experiments. The method produces statistical and numerical information. It provides hard facts and figures, and uses statistics and numbers to draw conclusions and make an analysis.

Many researchers in the field of health and care use quantitative approaches and produce quantitative data. They may carry out 'experiments' using many of the rules of scientific investigation. In general, if you are reading research which provides statistics and numerical information and is based purely on facts, it is likely to have used one of the quantitative approaches.

Many government publications are good examples of quantitative research – they give statistics in relation to the National Health Service, for example, such as the numbers of patients on waiting lists, the numbers having a particular operation, or the numbers of residents in nursing homes throughout the country.

Qualitative research

A qualitative approach looks at the 'quality' rather than the 'quantity' of something. It would be used to investigate the feelings of people who have remained on the waiting list for treatment, or people's attitudes towards residential care, or the relationships between those in residential care and those who care for them. Generally, qualitative data is produced in words rather than figures and will consist of descriptions and information about people's lives, experiences and attitudes.

Active knowledge

By using any of the methods for finding up-to-date information, such as newspapers, journals, reports, television, the Internet or textbooks, find two pieces of research carried out within the past two years. One should be quantitative and one qualitative. Read the results of both pieces of research and make a note of the differences in the type of information provided.

How to ensure your practice is current and up to date

There is little point in reading articles, watching TV programmes and attending training days if your work practice is not updated and improved as a result. With the enormous pressures on everybody in the health and care services, it is often difficult to find time to keep up to date and to change the practices you are used to. Any form of change takes time and is always a little uncomfortable or unusual to begin with. So when we are under pressure because of the amount of work we have to do, it is only normal that we tend to rely on practices, methods and ways of working which are comfortable, familiar and can be done swiftly and efficiently.

You will need to make a very conscious effort to incorporate new learning into your practice. You need to allocate time to updating your knowledge, and incorporating it into your practice. You could try the following ways to ensure that you are using the new knowledge you have gained.

Keys to good practice: Applying new skills and knowledge in practice

✓ Plan out how you will adapt your practice on a day-to-day basis, adding one new aspect each day. Do this until you have covered all the aspects of the new information you have learned.

✓ Discuss with your supervisor and colleagues what you have learned and how you intend to change your practice, and ask for feedback.

✓ Write a checklist for yourself and check it at the end of each day.

✓ Give yourself a set period of time, for example one month, to alter or improve your practice, and review it at the end of that time.

New knowledge is not only about the most exciting emerging theories. It is also often about mundane and day-to-day aspects of your practice, which are just as important and can make just as much difference to the quality of care you provide for your service users. It is also about taking your practice forward by developing your knowledge across a range of situations.

CASE STUDY: Opportunities for self-directed training

Meena works as a care worker at a big, busy day centre and meets the families of service users of all ages. One day she was chatting to the daughter of a service user and mentioned the problem of teenage pregnancy, expressing her disapproval of the extreme youth of some new mothers. 'It's funny you should say that', replied the woman, 'but my daughter Louise is pregnant. I'm not that happy – she's only 16 – but what can you do?' Meena felt embarrassed, but decided she needed to be better informed on the issue. She got in touch with the local family planning clinic and spoke to the manager, explaining that she would like to learn more about the sexual health services available to young people. She arranged to spend some time on a self-directed 'work experience' placement at the clinic, and is now a volunteer there, helping to run the crèche. In her reflective diary she writes:

'Really tired tonight. All day at work and then 2 hours at the clinic. Spent half an hour with a young girl who was crying because her Dad has threatened to kick her out. Helped her fill in some forms and arrange to see social services. All this is making me more aware, and I hope a better all-round carer.'

1 *What benefits to Meena's 'day job' do you think will come from her self-directed training?*

2 *How can training help to overcome prejudice?*

Active knowledge

Think about an occasion when you have been able to reflect on an area of your own practice or knowledge which needed improvement, and the steps you took to achieve the improvement. Record what you did and also how you incorporated the new knowledge into your practice. Once you have identified this and recorded it in detail, you should include it in your NVQ portfolio as part of the evidence that you will need to achieve this unit.

Preparing a development plan

It is a requirement of many organisations that their staff have personal development plans. A personal development plan is a very important document as it identifies a worker's training and development needs and, because the plan is updated when the worker has taken part in training and development, it also provides a record of participation.

A personal development plan should be worked out with your supervisor, but it is essentially your plan for your career. You need to think about what you want to achieve, and discuss with your supervisor the best ways of achieving your goals.

There is no single right way to prepare a personal development plan, and each organisation is likely to have its own way. However, it should include different development areas, such as practical skills and communication skills, the goals or targets you have set – such as learning to manage a team – and a timescale for achieving them. Timescales must be realistic; for example, if you were to decide that you needed to achieve competence in managing a team in six months, this would be unrealistic and unachievable. You would inevitably fail to meet your target and would therefore be likely to become demoralised and demotivated. But if your target was to attend a training and development programme on team building during the next six months and to lead perhaps two team meetings by the end of the six months, those goals and targets would be realistic and you would be likely to achieve them.

When you have set your targets, you need to review how you are progressing towards achieving them – this should happen every six months or so. You need to look at what you have achieved and how your plan needs to be updated.

Development plans can take many forms, but the best ones are likely to be developed in conjunction with your manager or workplace supervisor. You need to carefully consider the 'areas of competence' and understand which ones you need to develop for your work role. Identify each as either an area in which you feel fully confident, one where there is room for improvement and development, or one where you have very limited current ability. The headings in the table on the next page are suggestions only.

Self-esteem has a major effect on people's health and well-being. People with a confident, positive view of themselves, who believe that they have value and worth, are far more likely to be happy and healthy than someone whose self-esteem is poor and whose confidence is low.

People who have a positive and confident outlook are far more likely to be interested and active in the world around them, while those lacking confidence and belief in their own abilities are more likely to be withdrawn and reluctant to try anything new. It is easy to see how this can affect someone's quality of life and reduce his or her overall health and well-being.

Empowerment for service users

It is often the case that individuals are told the level of support they will receive and the days on which they will receive it. They may even be told the times at which they will receive such help. The reasons for this are obvious: all services have limited budget and staff resources, and these have to be managed in order to provide the best possible service for the largest number of people. However, this leaves a circle to be squared. Organisations that plan and deliver services have to respond on a general scale; they will try to take into account individual needs, but the nature of organisations makes it difficult to do so effectively.

The point at which practices can be adapted to meet needs and empower individuals, their families and carers, is when the care worker delivering the service meets and interacts with the individual. There are many ways in which you can ensure that your own practice empowers individuals as far as possible. These are discussed in detail on page 187.

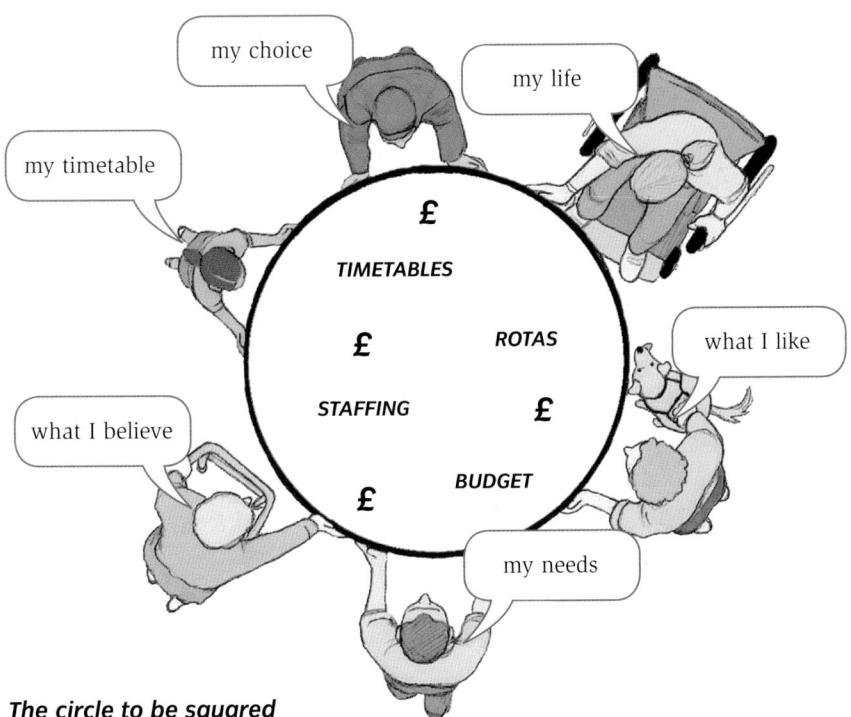

The circle to be squared

CASE STUDY: Empowerment

Reg is 82, and lives with his wife Enid. Although she is slow to get around, Enid still manages most domestic chores and personal care.

Reg has been diagnosed with the early stages of Azheimer's disease, and he and Enid are aware that their way of life might change in the future. They have been receiving help twice a week with the cleaning and ironing, but after talking to Doreen, their support worker, the care manager decides to discuss the idea of putting in more support for Reg and Enid now, in order to avoid crises in the future.

1 *How should the care manager move the discussion forward in order to support Reg and Enid?*

2 *What additional support organisations could Reg access?*

3 *A diagnosis of Alzheimer's disease has frightening connotations for many people. How could the care manager address such fears sensitively as well as practically?*

Active knowledge

Using the list you made for the activity on page 167, make notes about the differences which could be made to the life of each individual you work with if he or she was able to make the choices you have identified.

Individuals' rights

Rights and responsibilities are a huge subject. In order to look at rights in terms of how they affect the people you work with and provide care for, it is helpful to discuss them under the following headings:

- rights under National Standards, codes of practice, charters, guidelines and policies
- rights provided by law.

Responsibilities are the other side of the coin to rights – most of our responsibilities are about protecting, improving or not infringing other people's rights. Responsibilities are the balance for rights, and it is impossible to consider one without the other.

Rights under codes, charters, guidelines and policies

These are rights which do not have the force of law, but which are enforceable within care work and designed to improve the services people receive.

National Minimum Standards

The Commission for Social Care Inspection (CSCI) now has responsibility for inspecting care services, and it is planned that this commission will take over the inspection of health services in the future. The CSCI uses a series of National Minimum Standards in order to inspect the quality of care. There are different sets of standards for different types of services. For example,

Did you know?

The CSCI has produced a booklet entitled 'Care Homes for Older People' detailing the rights that older people have within a care home. These rights include:

- privacy and dignity
- choice and control
- the meeting of cultural and spiritual needs
- health and well-being
- a social life and activities
- good food
- a clean, comfortable and safe home
- protection from harm and abuse.

Full details of national standards and booklets for service users can be found at www.csci.org.uk.

there are standards for care homes for older people, separate standards for care homes for younger adults, for children's homes and for fostering services. The standards documents provide a detailed set of definitions that outline the minimum quality of care that a service user may expect.

National Minimum Standards documents may appear rather technical; for example the standards for care homes for older people are 42 pages long plus appendices, and are intended to provide clear definitions to define quality care for inspection purposes. But the CSCI has now started to produce easy-to-read documents intended for service users.

Codes of practice

In 2002 the General Social Care Council published a code of practice for both employees and employers. A summary of the code of practice for employees is set out below.

Duties under the GSCC Code of Practice for Social Care Workers	
Protect the rights and promote the interests of service users and care workers Respect for **individuality** and support for service users to control their own lives. Respect for and maintenance of **equal opportunities, diversity,** dignity and privacy.	**Promote the independence of service users while protecting them from danger or harm** Maintenance of **rights**, challenging and reporting dangerous, abusive, discriminatory, or exploitative behaviour. Following **safe** practice, reporting resource problems, reporting unsafe practice of colleagues, following **health and safety regulations**, helping service users to make complaints and using **power** responsibly.
Establish and maintain the trust and confidence of service users Maintaining **confidentiality**, using effective **communication**, honouring commitments and agreements, declaring conflicts of interest and adhering to policies about accepting gifts.	**Respect the rights of service users while seeking to ensure that their behaviour does not harm themselves or other people** Recognising the right to take **risks**, following risk assessment policies, minimising risks, ensuring others are informed about risk assessments.
Uphold public trust and confidence in social care services Not abusing, neglecting or exploiting service users or colleagues, or forming inappropriate personal relationships. Not **discriminating** or condoning discrimination, or placing self or others at unnecessary **risk**. Not abusing the trust of others in relation to **confidentiality**.	**Be accountable for the quality of your work and take responsibility for maintaining and improving your knowledge and skills** Meeting standards, maintaining appropriate records and informing employers of personal difficulties. Seeking assistance and co-operating with colleagues, recognising responsibility for delegated work, respecting the roles of others and undertaking **relevant training**.

If you supervise other staff you may also need to consider the GSCC code of practice for employers, a summary of which is set out on the next page:

Code of Practice for Employers of Social Care Workers

1 Employers must make sure people are suitable to enter the social care work force and understand their roles and responsibilities.

2 Employers must have written policies and procedures in place to enable social care workers to meet the GSCC's Code of Practice for Social Care Workers. This includes written policies on:
- confidentiality
- equal opportunities
- risk assessment
- record keeping
- acceptance of gifts
- substance abuse.

Employers must also provide:
- effective systems of management and supervision
- systems to report inadequate resources
- support for workers to meet the GSCC code of practice.

3 Employers must provide training and development opportunities to enable social care workers to strengthen and develop their skills and knowledge, including:
- induction
- workplace assessment and practice learning
- supporting staff to meet eligibility criteria
- responding to workers who seek assistance.

4 Employers must put into place and implement written policies and procedures to deal with dangerous, discriminatory or exploitative behaviour and practice, including written policies and procedures on:
- bullying, harassment and discrimination
- procedures to report dangerous, discriminatory, abusive or exploitative behaviour
- policies to minimise the risk of violence and to manage violent incidents
- support for workers who experience trauma or violence
- equal opportunities
- assistance to care workers in relation to health needs.

5 Employers must promote the GSCC's codes of practice to social care workers, service users and carers and co-operate with the GSCC's proceedings. This includes informing workers of the code, informing social care users, using the code to assist in decision making, informing the GSCC of any misconduct, and co-operating with the GSCC in investigations.

If you supervise staff you may need to consider the GSCC code of practice for employers

The table below lists some service-user rights, based on the GSCC Code of Practice.

Moral rights of service users	GSCC standards
Diversity and respect for differences	1.1 treating each person as an individual 1.2 respecting and promoting individual views 1.6 respecting diversity and different cultures and values
Equality in care practice	1.5 promoting equal opportunities
Anti-discriminatory practice	5.5 not discriminating 5.6 not condoning discrimination
Confidentiality	2.3 respecting confidential information
Control over own life, choice and independence	1.3 supporting service users' rights to control their lives and make informed choices 3.1 promoting the independence of service users 3.7 helping service users and care workers to make complaints 3.8 recognising and using power responsibly
Dignity and privacy	1.4 respecting and maintaining the dignity and privacy of service users
Effective communication	2.2 communicating in an appropriate, open, accurate and straightforward way
Safety and security	Principle 3 promotes independence while protecting service users, including health and safety policies; appropriate practice and procedures 4.2/4.3 following risk assessment policies, taking steps to minimise risk 5.2 not exploiting service users 5.7 not putting self or others at risk
Right to take risks	4.1 helping service users to identify and manage risks

Your employer will have a range of policy and procedure documents that will also define how staff should behave towards service users.

Evidence indicator

The organisation you work for will have policies and statements about rights. Find out what they are, and see how you feel your workplace measures up to its stated aims, mission statements and required standards of care. Keep your notes for your portfolio.

Rights also involve responsibilities. Everyone has the responsibility not to infringe the rights of other people. Some responsibilities linked to the rights above are set out below:

Rights of service users	Responsibilities
Diversity and the right to be different Including an individual's right to express his or her own identity, culture, lifestyle and interpretation of life.	**Respect for diversity in others** Including an acceptance that other people have a right to interpret life differently. A responsibility not to discriminate against others on the basis that the individual's identity, lifestyle or culture is morally superior to that of others.
Equality and freedom from discrimination Including freedom from discrimination on the basis of race, sex, ability, sexuality or religion.	**Respect for the equality of others** Including respect for, and not discrimination against, members of other social groups.
Control over own life, choice and independence Including the freedom to choose lifestyle, self-presentation, diet and routine.	**Respect for the independence, choice and lifestyle of others** Including arriving at a balance between the impact of the individual's own choices and the needs of other people who may be affected by them – including care workers.
Dignity and privacy Including the right to be responded to in terms of the service user's own interpretation of dignity and respect.	**Respect for the dignity and privacy of others** Including issues associated with the identity needs of other users or carers.
Confidentiality Including rights as established in law and codes of practice.	**Respect for the confidentiality of others** Including others' legal rights, and rights established in codes of practice.
Effective communication Including appropriately clear and supportive communication that minimises vulnerability.	**Communication with others which does not seek to cause offence or threaten**

Continued

Rights of service users	Responsibilities
Safety and security Including physical safety, living in an environment that promotes health and emotional safety, security of property, and freedom from physical, social, emotional or economic abuse.	**Contributing to the safety and security of others** Including behaving in a way that does not threaten or abuse the physical or emotional safety and security of others.
The right to take risks Including taking risks as a matter of choice, in order to maintain the service user's own identity or perceived well-being.	**Not to expose oneself or others to unacceptable risks** Including a willingness to negotiate with respect to the impact of risk on others.

Rights provided by law

Most of the provisions of the UK's Human Rights Act came into force on 2 October 2000. This means that residents of the United Kingdom – this Act applies in England, Scotland, Wales and Northern Ireland – will now be entitled to seek help from the courts if they believe that their human rights have been infringed.

Organisations subject to Human Rights Act 1998	
Residential homes or nursing homes	These perform functions which would otherwise be performed by a local authority
Charities	
Voluntary organisations	
Public services	This could include the privatised utilities, such as gas, electric and water companies

It is likely that anyone who works in health or care will be working within the provisions of the Human Rights Act, which guarantees the following rights.

1 The right to life.

2 The right to freedom from torture and inhuman or degrading treatment or punishment.

3 The right to freedom from slavery, servitude and forced or compulsory labour.

4 The right to liberty and security of person.

5 The right to a fair and public trial within a reasonable time.

6   The right to freedom from retrospective criminal law and no punishment without law.

7   The right to respect for private and family life, home and correspondence.

8   The right to freedom of thought, conscience and religion.

9   The right to freedom of expression.

10 The right to freedom of assembly and association.

11 The right to marry and found a family.

12 The prohibition of discrimination in the enjoyment of convention rights.

13 The right to peaceful enjoyment of possessions and protection of property.

14 The right of access to an education.

15 The right of free elections.

16 The right not to be subjected to the death penalty.

Law, rights and discrimination

Discrimination is a denial of rights. Discrimination can be based on issues such as race, gender, disability or sexual orientation. The main Acts of Parliament which are related to discrimination are:

- the Equal Pay Act 1970
- the Sex Discrimination Act 1975 (amended 1986)
- the Race Relations Act 1976 (amended 2000)
- the Disability Discrimination Act 1995 and Disability Rights Commission Act 1999.

In addition it is important to note the regulations that provide a legal right not to be discriminated against on the basis of sexual orientation or religious belief. These are:

- Employment Equality (Sexual Orientation) Regulations 2003
- Employment Equality (Religion or Belief) Regulations 2003

Equal Pay Act 1970

This Act made it unlawful for employers to discriminate between men and women in terms of their pay and conditions of work. Before this law was passed it was possible for an employer to pay men more than women – even though they were doing the same job!

Equal pay legislation was updated in 1975 and 1983 to make it possible to claim equal pay for work that was considered to be of 'equal value'.

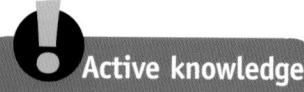
Active knowledge

As you consider these Acts of Parliament, make notes on whether your workplace and your own practice fully support this legislation. Be as critical as necessary. If there are gaps or problems with compliance, how could you make your workplace into a more anti-discriminatory environment? What could you do as your personal contribution?

Did you know?

Average male wages in the UK are still about 20 per cent higher than women's. In 1965, women's average wage was half that of men.

Sex Discrimination Act 1975

This Act made it unlawful to discriminate between men and women in respect of employment, goods and facilities. The Act also made it illegal to discriminate on the grounds of marital status. The Act identified two forms of discrimination: direct discrimination and indirect discrimination.

The Act tries to provide equal opportunities for men and women in getting jobs and promotion. In order to make sure that people's rights were protected, the government set up the **Equal Opportunities Commission** to monitor, advise and provide information on men and women's rights under the law. The commission will give help and advice to people who believe they have been discriminated against because of their gender. The law was updated in 1986 so that it also applies to small businesses.

Race Relations Act 1976

This Act makes it unlawful to discriminate on 'racial grounds' in employment, housing or services. This includes colour, race, nationality, ethnic or national origins. The Act makes it an offence to incite or encourage racial hatred. As in the law against sex discrimination, both direct and indirect discrimination are targeted.

The **Commission for Racial Equality** was set up in 1976 to make sure that the law against racial discrimination works. The commission can investigate cases of discrimination and give advice to people who wish to take legal action because of discrimination. The law was strengthened and widened by an amendment in 2000 in order to prevent discrimination in any public situation.

Active knowledge

Research the work of the Commission for Racial Equality and see whether you can find any recent cases relating to health and social care workers. Do they include any issues that could occur in your workplace?

Disability Discrimination Act 1995

This Act is designed to prevent discrimination against people with disabilities in employment, access to education and transport, housing and obtaining goods and services. Employers and landlords must not treat a disabled person less favourably than a non-disabled person. New transport facilities must meet the needs of disabled people and colleges, shops and other services must ensure that disabled people can use their services.

The **Disability Rights Commission** was set up by the Disability Rights Commission Act, 1999. This commission has the power to conduct formal investigations and to serve non-discrimination notices, make agreements, and take other action to prevent discrimination against people with a disability. The commission can give advice to people who believe they have experienced discrimination.

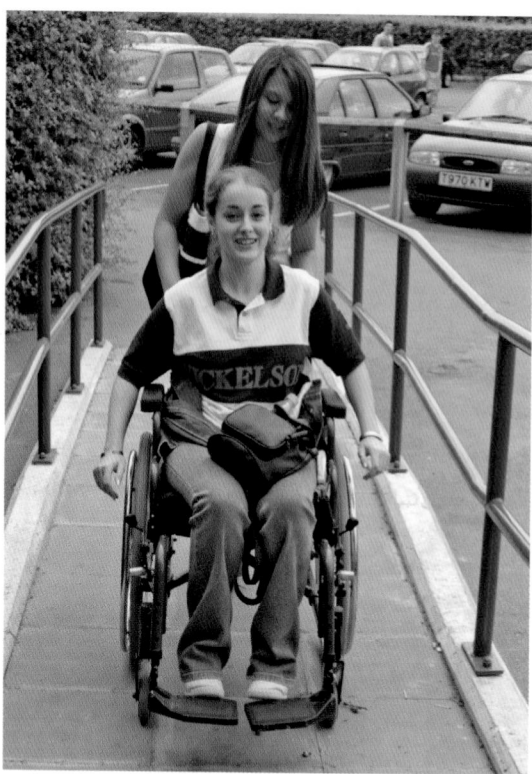

Disabled people need to be able to access premises and facilities

Providing support to meet the needs and preferences of individuals

Some service users may perceive themselves as vulnerable because they feel that they cannot control the extent to which their needs are likely to be met. Some people with a learning difficulty may perceive themselves as dependent on their care workers to organise appropriate daily activities to ensure their needs are met. Some older service users may be disorientated, and people with dementia may feel that they are unable to interpret and control their surroundings without appropriate support. Children are often unable to make wise decisions or choices because of limited understanding of the world. Children may often have to rely on adult guidance in order to be safe.

As well as vulnerability with respect to needs, service users can also be at risk of exploitation, abuse and physical or emotional damage resulting from unmet needs. It is therefore vitally important that care workers are actively concerned with promoting choice and independence in all their interactions with service users.

Maslow's hierarchy of needs

A widely accepted model for interpreting human needs was developed by Abraham Maslow. Although Maslow's hierarchy may be perceived as a simplification, it provides a useful tool for summarising the range of human needs. There was a time when care was thought of as being about only the

CASE STUDY: Dealing with prejudice

Garth is a care worker in a residential setting for adults with disabilities. He is gay but had never discussed his sexual orientation at work and it was not mentioned at the time of his appointment. His sexual orientation only became known when the parents of one of the residents spotted him in a photograph of a gay pride event printed in a national newspaper.

Garth had always been a popular member of staff and had an excellent work record, with appraisals which showed his skills and abilities were developing and progressing. However, following the discovery that he was gay the atmosphere in the setting began to change. Two of the residents complained about being cared for by someone who was gay and said they were not prepared to have Garth provide them with any personal care. Both of these residents were young men in their late 20s and their action was supported by their parents. Comments and jokes at Garth's expense began to circulate within the setting, particularly when Garth was on duty.

Garth felt that he was unfairly discriminated against and intended to obtain the support of his trade union.

1 *What are Garth's rights in this situation? Consider the Employment Equality (Sexual Orientation) Regulations.*

2 *What are the residents' rights? Consider the issue of rights and responsibilities.*

Test yourself

1 List at least three aspects of daily living where individuals may want to express a choice.

2 What would you do if someone told a racist joke:

   a laugh because it's only fun?

   b say nothing but feel awkward?

   c say that you find the joke offensive?

   Explain your answer.

3 Name three groups of people who are discriminated against.

4 What forms does the discrimination take?

5 How would you attempt to reduce the discrimination in those three instances?

6 What is stereotyping? Give an example.

HSC 35c Contribute to the protection of all individuals

In this element you will look at some of the most difficult issues that you will face as a care professional. For many people, starting work in care means coming to terms with the fact that some individuals will be subjected to abuse by those who are supposed to care for them. For others it will not be the first time that they have been close to an abuse situation, either through personal or previous professional involvement.

Regardless of previous experience, coming face to face with situations where abuse is, or has been, taking place is difficult and emotionally demanding. Knowing what you are looking for, and how to recognise it, is an important part of ensuring that you are making the best possible contribution to protecting individuals from abuse. You need to know how society handles abuse, how to recognise it, and what to do about it. It is a tragic fact that almost all disclosures of abuse are true – and you will have to learn to *think the unthinkable*.

The forms of abuse which you will need to be aware of and to understand are abuses which are suffered by individuals at the hands of someone who is providing care for them – abusers can be parents, informal carers, care professionals and/or the policies and practices of the care setting itself. (This element is not about abuse by strangers, which needs to be dealt with in the same way as any other crime.) If you can learn always to consider the possibility of abuse, always to be alert to potentially abusive situations and always to *listen* and *believe* when you are told of abuse, then you will provide the best possible protection for the individuals you care for.

Taking the right steps when faced with an abusive situation is the second part of your key contribution to individuals who are being, or have been, abused.

Forms of abuse

Abuse can take many forms. These are usually classified under five main headings:
- physical
- sexual
- emotional
- financial
- institutional.

Abuse can happen to any individual regardless of his or her age or service needs. Child abuse is the most well-known and well-recognised type of abuse, but all service user groups can suffer abuse. Abuse of older people and abuse of people with learning difficulties, sensory impairment or physical disabilities is just as common, but often less well recognised.

Physical abuse

Any abuse involving the use of force is classified as physical abuse. This can mean:

- punching, hitting, slapping, pinching, kicking, in fact any form of physical attack
- burning or scalding
- restraint such as tying up or tying people to beds or furniture
- refusal to allow access to toilet facilities
- deliberate starvation or force feeding
- leaving individuals in wet or soiled clothing or bedding as a deliberate act to demonstrate the power and strength of the abuser
- excessive or inappropriate use of medication
- a carer causing illness or injury to someone he or she cares for in order to gain attention (this might be associated with a disorder called 'Munchausen's syndrome by proxy').

Remember

Abuse of vulnerable individuals can take many forms. An individual may be subjected to more than one type of abuse.

Sexual abuse

Sexual abuse, whether of adults or children, can also involve abuse of a position of power. Children can never be considered to give informed consent to any sexual activity of any description. For many adults, informed consent is not possible because of a limited understanding of the issues. In the case of other adults, consent may not be given and the sexual activity is either forced on the individual against his or her will or the individual is tricked or bribed into it.

Sexual activity is abusive when informed consent is not freely given. This might involve one service user abusing another more vulnerable service user. It is important to recognise the difference between the freely consenting sexual activity of adults who also happen to be service users, and those situations where abuse is taking place because someone is exploiting his or her position of relative power.

Sexual abuse can consist of:

- sexual penetration of any part of the body with a penis, finger or any object
- touching inappropriate parts of the body or any other form of sexual contact without the informed agreement of the individual
- sexual exploitation
- exposure to, or involvement in, pornographic or erotic material
- exposure to, or involvement in, sexual rituals
- making sexually related comments or references which provide sexual gratification for the abuser
- making threats about sexual activities.

Emotional abuse

All the other forms of abuse also have an element of emotional abuse. Any situation which means that an individual becomes a victim of abuse at the hands of someone he or she trusted is, inevitably, going to cause emotional distress. However, some abuse is purely emotional – there are no physical, sexual or financial elements involved. This abuse can take the form of:

- humiliation, belittling, putting down
- withdrawing or refusing affection
- bullying
- making threats
- shouting or swearing
- making insulting or abusive remarks
- racial abuse
- constant teasing and poking fun.

Financial abuse

Many service users are very vulnerable to financial abuse, particularly those who may have a limited understanding of money matters. Financial abuse, like all other forms of abuse, can be inflicted by family members and even friends as well as care workers or informal carers, and can take a range of forms, such as:

- stealing money or property
- allowing or encouraging others to steal money or property
- tricking or threatening individuals into giving away money or property
- persuading individuals to take financial decisions which are not in their interests
- withholding money, or refusing access to money
- refusing to allow individuals to manage their own financial affairs
- failing to support individuals to manage their own financial affairs.

Institutional abuse

Institutional abuse is not only confined to large-scale physical or sexual abuse scandals of the type which are regularly publicised in the media. Of course this type of systematic and organised abuse goes on in residential and hospital settings, and must be recognised and dealt with appropriately so that service users can be protected. However, individuals can be abused in many other ways in settings where they could expect to be cared for and protected. For example:

- individuals in residential settings are not given choice over day-to-day decisions such as mealtimes, bedtimes, etc.
- freedom to go out is limited by the institution
- privacy and dignity are not respected
- personal correspondence is opened by staff

- the setting is run for the convenience of staff, not service users
- excessive or inappropriate doses of sedation/medication are given
- access to advice and advocacy is restricted or not allowed
- complaints procedures are deliberately made unavailable.

You can probably begin to see that the different types of abuse are often interlinked, and individuals can be victims of more than one type of abuse. Abuse may be a deliberate act – something which someone actively does in order to demonstrate power and authority over another person. Abuse can also be motivated by the abuser deriving pleasure from his or her actions.

Neglect

Neglect happens when care is not given and an individual suffers as a result. The whole area of neglect has many aspects you need to take into account, but there are broadly two different types of neglect:
- self-neglect
- neglect by others.

Self-neglect

Many people neglect themselves; this can be for a range of reasons. People may be ill or depressed and unable to make the effort, or not feel capable of looking after themselves. Sometimes people feel that looking after themselves is unimportant. Others choose to live in a way that does not match up to the expectations of other people. Working out when someone is neglecting himself or herself, given all of these considerations, can be very difficult.

Self-neglect can show itself in a range of ways:

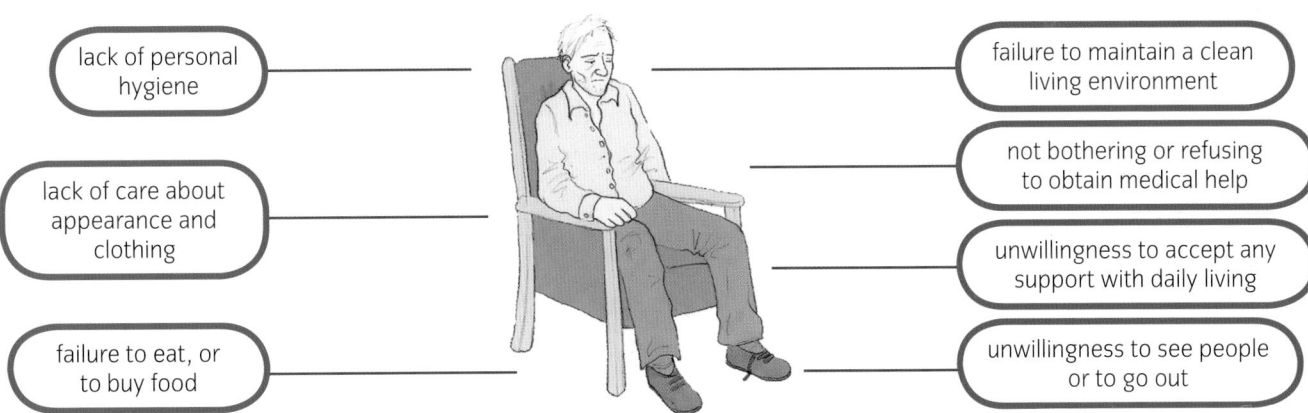

lack of personal hygiene

lack of care about appearance and clothing

failure to eat, or to buy food

failure to maintain a clean living environment

not bothering or refusing to obtain medical help

unwillingness to accept any support with daily living

unwillingness to see people or to go out

However, what may appear to be self-neglect may, in fact, be an informed choice made by someone who does not regard personal and domestic cleanliness or hygiene as priorities. It is always important to make a professional judgement based on talking with the individual and finding out his or her wishes, before making any assumptions about what may be needed.

Neglect by others

This occurs when either a care worker or an informal carer fails to meet the care needs of a person. Neglect can happen because those responsible for providing the care do not realise its importance, or because they cannot be bothered, or choose not, to provide it. As the result of neglect, individuals can become ill, hungry, cold, dirty, injured or deprived of their rights. Neglecting someone you are supposed to be caring for can mean failing to undertake a range of care services, for example:

- not providing adequate food
- not providing assistance with eating food if necessary
- not ensuring that the individual receives personal care
- not ensuring that the individual is adequately clothed
- leaving the individual alone
- not assisting an individual to meet mobility or communication needs
- failing to maintain a clean and hygienic living environment
- failing to obtain necessary medical/health-care support
- not supporting social contacts
- not taking steps to provide a safe and secure environment for the individual.

Remember

Neglect occurs when a person's needs are not being met.

In some care situations, care workers may fail to provide some aspects of care because they have not been trained, or because they work in a setting where the emphasis is on cost saving rather than care provision. In these circumstances it becomes a form of institutional abuse. Unfortunately, there have been residential care homes and NHS trusts where individuals have been found to be suffering from malnutrition as the result of such neglect. Individual workers who are deliberately neglecting service users in spite of receiving training and working in a quality caring environment are, fortunately, likely to be spotted very quickly by colleagues and supervisors.

However, carers who are supporting individuals in their own homes are in different circumstances, often facing huge pressures and difficulties. Some may be reluctantly caring for a relative because they feel they have no choice; others may be barely coping with their own lives and may find caring for someone else a burden they are unable to bear. Regardless of the many possible reasons for the difficulties which can result in neglect, it is essential that a suspicion of neglect is investigated and that concerns are followed up so that help can be offered and additional support provided if necessary.

As with self-neglect, it is important that lifestyle decisions made by individuals and their carers are respected, and full discussions should take place with individuals and carers where there are concerns about possible neglect.

How the law affects what you do

Much of the work in caring is governed by legislation, but the only group where legislation specifically provides for protection from abuse is children. Older people and people with a learning disability, physical disabilities or mental health problems have service provision, rights and many other requirements laid down in law, but no overall legal framework to provide protection from abuse.

The laws which cover your work in the field of care are summarised in the table below.

Service user group	Laws that govern their care	Protection from abuse
Children	Children Act 1989	Yes
People with mental health problems	Mental Health Act 1983 (draft Mental Health Bill 2004)	No
Adults with learning disabilities	Mental Health Act 1983	No
Adults with disabilities	Chronically Sick and Disabled Persons Act 1986 Disability Discrimination Act 1995	No
Older people	National Assistance Act 1948 NHS Community Care Act 1990	No
All service user groups	Care Standards Act 2000	Yes, through raising standards

There are, however, a number of sets of guidelines, policies and procedures in respect of abuse for service user groups other than children, and you will need to ensure that you are familiar with policies for your area of work and particularly with those policies which apply in your own workplace.

Dealing with abuse is difficult and demanding for everyone, and it is essential that you receive professional supervision from your manager. This may be undertaken in a regular supervision or support meeting if you have one; if not, it will be important that you arrange to meet with your supervisor so that you can ensure you are working in the correct way and in accordance with the procedure in your setting.

Your supervisor will also need to be assured that you are coping on a personal and professional level with the effects of having to deal with an abusive situation.

Active knowledge

Ask your supervisor about the procedures in your workplace for dealing with abuse. There should be a written policy and guidelines to be followed if abuse is suspected. Ask if there are any laws or guidelines that relate to the way you work. Check with experienced colleagues about situations they have dealt with and ask them to tell you about what happened.

Government policies and guidelines

The most important set of government guidelines which lays down practices for co-operation between agencies is called 'Working Together to Safeguard Children'. It was published in 1999 and forms the basis for child-protection work. This guideline ensures that information is shared between agencies and professionals, and that decisions in respect of children are not taken by just one person.

A similar set of guidelines has been published by the government about adults, called 'No Secrets'. These guidelines state that older people have specific rights, which include being treated with respect, and being able to live in their home and community without fear of physical or emotional violence or harassment.

The guidance gives local authorities the lead responsibility in co-ordinating the procedures. Each local authority area must have a multi-agency management committee for the protection of vulnerable adults, which will develop policies, protocols and practices. The guidance covers:

- identification of those at risk
- setting up an inter-agency framework
- developing inter-agency policy – procedures for responding in individual cases
- recruitment, training and other staff and management issues.

A government White Paper published in 2001, 'Valuing People: A New Strategy for Learning Disability in the 21st Century', sets out the ways in which services for people with a learning disability will be improved. 'Valuing People' sets out four main principles for service provision for people with a learning disability:

- civil rights
- independence
- choice
- inclusion.

The White Paper also makes it clear that people with a learning disability are entitled to the full protection of the law.

Recent policy approaches to protecting children and vulnerable adults in care environments have concentrated on improving and monitoring the quality of the service provided to them. The principle behind this is that if the overall quality of practice in care is constantly improved, then well-trained staff working to high standards are less likely to abuse service users, and are more likely to identify and deal effectively with any abuse they find.

What does the law say about protecting children?

The Children Act 1989 requires that local authority social services departments provide protection from abuse for children in their area. The Act of Parliament gives powers to social services departments, following the procedures laid down by the Area Child Protection Committee, to take legal steps to ensure the safety of children.

What does the law say about protecting vulnerable adults?

The Acts of Parliament that are mainly concerned with provisions for vulnerable adults are the National Assistance Act 1948 and the NHS and Community Care Act 1990. They do not specifically give social services departments a 'duty to protect' but, of course, people are protected by the law. If a vulnerable adult is abused and that abuse is considered to be a criminal offence, then the police will act. It is sometimes thought that because someone is confused, a prosecution will not be brought – this is not so. All vulnerable adults will have the full protection of the law if any criminal offences are committed.

The Mental Health Act 1983 (and the draft Mental Health Bill) forms the framework for service provision for people with mental health problems or a learning disability. There are provisions within this legislation for social services departments to assume responsibility for people who are so 'mentally impaired' that they are not able to be responsible for their own affairs. This is called guardianship. However, like all other vulnerable adults, there is no specific duty to protect people from abuse.

'Valuing People' (see page 220) forms the basis for services to all people with a learning disability and provides rights, but no specific duty of protection.

While the Chronically Sick and Disabled Persons Act and the Disability Discrimination Act provide disabled people with rights, services and protection from discrimination, they do not provide any means of comprehensive protection from abuse.

As with all vulnerable groups, there is a long and tragic history to the physical and emotional abuse suffered by people with physical disabilities or a learning disability. The public humiliation and abuse of those with mental health problems is still visible today, so it is hardly surprising that abuse on an individual level is still all too commonplace.

Did you know?

The Protection of Vulnerable Adults – POVA – scheme for England and Wales, published by the Department of Health in 2004, aims to prevent those professionals who have harmed vulnerable adults in their care from taking up employment in the sector. It adds an extra layer of protection to the pre-employment processes, including Criminal Records Bureau checks, which already take place and stop known abusers from entering the care workforce.

Information on ways to protect individuals

Safeguarding and protecting vulnerable adults and children is an area of work that has been in the public eye for many years. As a result of this, a great deal of research has been carried out, and plenty of information is available in order to develop and improve your understanding of this difficult subject. You will be able to find training courses available in your local area – all social services departments provide training by their specialists, and many private agencies with specialist knowledge, such as the NSPCC and Action on Elder Abuse, produce very useful training materials and publications.

Your supervisor or manager will be able to advise you about the best way to find out information, and you should choose the way in which you find it easiest to learn – you may prefer to attend a training course, to read a book or to watch a training video. Ask your supervisor to find out what is available in your workplace.

Following the rules

Much of what you read about dealing with abuse may give you the impression that this is a subject full of rules and procedures. It is, and for very good reasons. Abuse is extremely serious – it is potentially life-threatening. Systems and rules have been developed by learning from the tragedies that have happened in the past. Many of these tragedies occurred because procedures were either not in place, or were not followed. You must make sure that you and any staff you supervise know what the procedure is in your workplace and follow it carefully.

Test yourself

1   What are the signs of financial abuse?

2   What factors may lead you to consider that a carer is abusing an individual?

3   What is the difference between abuse and neglect?

4   Why is it important to record information about suspected or actual abuse?

5   What is your position if an individual asks you not to tell anyone about abuse he or she has experienced?

6   What are the two key things to do when someone discloses that he or she has been abused?

someone who receives a £1.20 per week increase in Income Support will not! Both, however, have experienced a change in their financial circumstances.

Similarly, someone who changes from working two days each week to a full-time job experiences a significant change which will involve alterations in the care package he or she receives. But someone who changes from working two days each week as a telephonist to working the same two days as a receptionist is unlikely to need significant changes in any care package.

CASE STUDY: Acknowledging change

Miss Pugh is aged 73. She lives alone and is a retired floor manager from a large local department store. She has had support from the home help and mobile meals service since her mobility deteriorated with the increasing severity of her arthritis over the last five years. She was a fiercely independent lady who had always refused to accept any benefits or support in addition to her state pension. After finally getting her agreement to review her finances, her key worker had identified that she had some additional benefits due to her from her company pension scheme. This had increased Miss Pugh's monthly income considerably and had eased her financial situation. However, this change in circumstances had also put her income above the payment threshold for home-help service and she now has to pay for the service that she had previously received at no charge. Miss Pugh is angry at this and is considering cancelling the home-help service, although she would find it extremely difficult to manage without it.

1   *How would you explain the situation to Miss Pugh?*

2   *What are the skills you would need in order to successfully encourage Miss Pugh to continue using support services?*

3   *Should such a possibility have been discussed with Miss Pugh in advance of obtaining her agreement to review her finances?*

Active knowledge

Look at your own circumstances over the past 10 years and make a list of the ways in which they have changed. For example, you may have more children than you had 10 years ago, or some children may have left home and moved away. Members of your family may have died or been born in the past 10 years, you could be living in a larger or a smaller house, you could have more money or less money, you could be doing a different job. All these are major changes which have taken place in your life in just the short period of 10 years. Listing them will help you see the types of situations that change and affect people's lives.

Then take a much shorter period, for example the past year, and look at much smaller changes which may have happened to you during that time. They could be changes in your finances and your job role. You could now be undertaking a qualification, you may be driving a different car, you may have acquired digital television – any number of small changes have affected the way you are living your life. Again, make a list of these changes and consider the impact each of them has had. Although the second list may have had a smaller impact than some of the big changes you listed in your first reflection, they will nonetheless have combined to bring about some quite significant changes in your lifestyle.

Consider the results of this exercise when you are thinking about the importance of contributing to the monitoring of care programmes which are in place for people you work with.

Possible changes in service users' circumstances

There are many aspects of service users' lives that could change. Some examples are shown below.

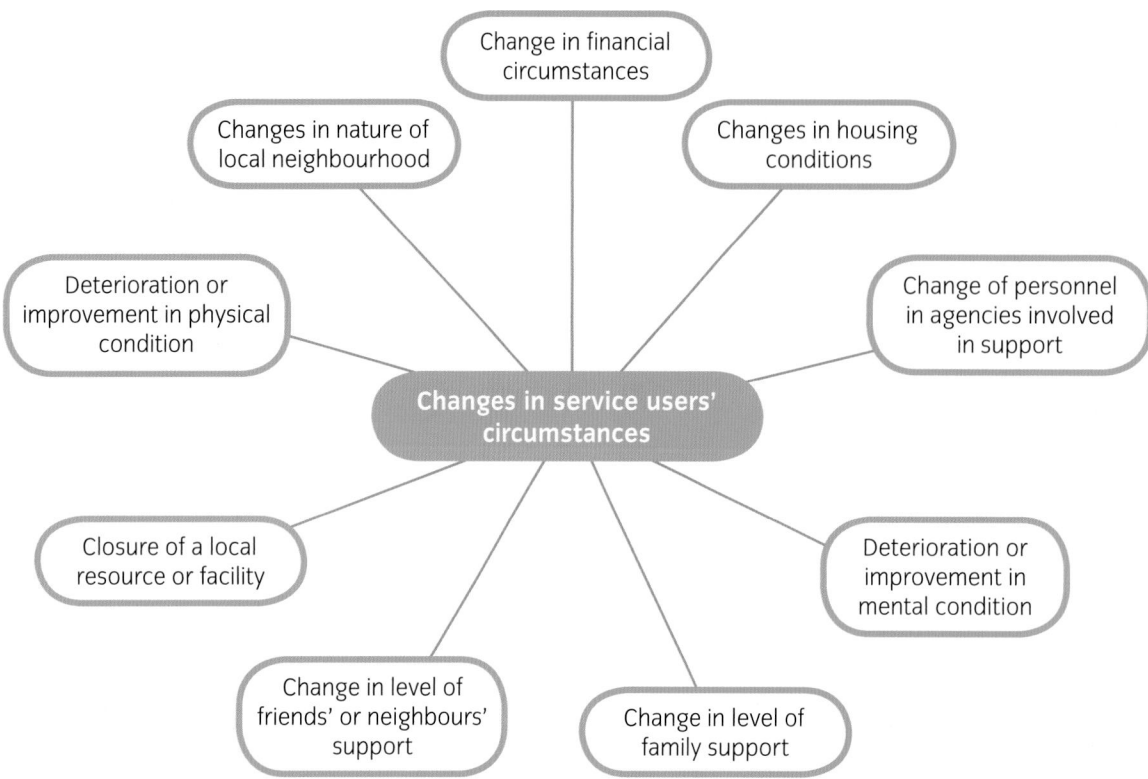

CASE STUDY: Changing levels of support

Katherine is a woman in her early 50s. She has Parkinson's disease, her level of mobility has been decreasing gradually over the past three years, and she has recently begun to fall frequently. She lives with her two sons aged 19 and 25, and her only contact with health and care provision so far has been through her hospital consultant and the primary care team. Her service requirements have been mainly medical with regular support from a physiotherapist.

Her increase in falling has coincided with a major change in her circumstances. Her younger son has been offered a place at an excellent university and her older son has been headhunted for his dream job in the United States on a two-year contract. Katherine does not want either of her sons to miss the opportunities they have been offered – so she now wants to discuss the ways in which she can arrange support that will allow her to remain as independent as possible.

1   *Who should be the first professionals Katherine holds discussions with?*

2   *Who else should be involved in planning?*

3   *How would you help to ensure that Katherine retained control of the process?*

4   *What feelings would you anticipate Katherine would have about her change in circumstances?*

5   *What steps do you think should be taken to make sure that Katherine remains independent?*

Keys to good practice: Developing and implementing care plans

✔ Support the individual in making a direct contribution to the process of planning his or her own care programme, and in expressing preferences.

✔ Check that proposals made by professional agencies meet with the agreement of the individual before starting any programme of care.

✔ Ensure that you are able to carry out the care plan activities for which you are responsible.

✔ Support colleagues to carry out the care plan activities for which they are responsible.

✔ Make arrangements to regularly feed back on the provision of the service.

✔ Contribute to arrangements for regularly reviewing the service and make sure that the individual is involved throughout the process.

Test yourself

1 What are the main points to remember about your role in developing and implementing care plans for the individuals you work with?

2 List three ways in which you could support individuals to comment on the content of the care plan.

3 Why is it important to monitor plans of care?

4 Describe three ways in which you could monitor a plan of care, and suggest the circumstances in which you would use the different methods.

5 What are some of the changes that could be made to a care plan as a result of monitoring?

HSC 328c Contribute to reviewing care plans

The purpose of reviews

Reviews are essential because care situations very rarely remain the same for long periods of time. As circumstances change, the package of care may need to be reviewed in the light of those changes. At agreed intervals, all of the parties involved should come together to reflect on whether or not the package of care is continuing to do the job it was initially set up to do. If there were no reviews, the arrangements could continue for years regardless of whether they were still meeting care needs.

A review will gather together all the information about the circumstances of the individual, the service provided and the service provider. It will give all those concerned with the care of the individual the opportunity to express their opinions and to be involved in a discussion about how effective care provision has been and the changes, if any, that need to be made.

The review process

Any review should attempt to obtain the views of as many people as possible who are involved in the care of the individual. The most important people at the review are the individual and his or her carers or family. You, as the person (or one of the people) providing services from the plan of care, are a very important contributor. The key worker or care manager/co-ordinator is also central to the review process, as is any organisation providing the care.

It is also important that others with an interest in the care of the individual have the opportunity to participate in a review. For example, a GP, health visitor, community psychiatric nurse, community occupational therapist, physiotherapist, speech therapist, welfare rights support worker, representative of a support group, or anyone else who has been a significant contributor to the life and care of the individual concerned should be involved if at all possible. The status of all the participants should be equal, in that everyone has the opportunity to give a view and to contribute to the discussion. However, the key person who must agree to any review decision is the individual concerned.

Remember

Nothing stays the same – everything is subject to change. This includes all aspects of people's circumstances. You must make sure that the care people receive changes in line with any changes in their lives.

People who might be involved in a review

How the review process is managed

The care manager/co-ordinator or key worker is likely to be the person responsible for organising the review itself and making sure that it takes place at the appropriate time. If the individual receiving care is receiving direct payment, he or she is likely to take responsibility for initiating a review if it is felt to be necessary. Where direct payments are involved your role is very different; it is simply one of being there to provide support and assistance if it is required by the individual. You would only become involved in a review if that was requested by the individual.

The person managing the review is likely to go through a checklist similar to the one below to make sure that the review meets the needs of the individual concerned.

Review checklist

1   Does the individual understand what a review is?

2   Do the individual's carers also understand what a review is and its purpose?

3   Is the review arranged at an appropriate time to check progress?

4   Is this an annual review or has it been triggered by a change in the individual's circumstances?

5   Does the review cover whether the individual continues to need the same level of support and services, whether there have been any changes, what the original care plan intended, and the results of monitoring?

6   Has the individual been asked when and where would be convenient for the review?

7   Has it been explained to the individual which decisions the review is able to take in respect of his or her continuing care provision and the development of a new care plan?

8   Has the individual been offered an advocate in order to help him or her prepare for the review, to support or to speak for him or her at the review?

9   Does the individual know who is responsible for making sure that the review meeting is managed?

10   Does the individual know all of the people who will be at the review?

11   Can all of the participants contribute either in writing or verbally to the review?

12   Do all the participants in the care plan know that they can request a review?

13   Have carers been consulted about the appropriate time and location for the review?

14   Have crèche facilities been offered for anyone who needs them so that they can attend the review?

During the review everyone should be given a chance to contribute. If the individual receiving care has chosen to use an advocate to present his or her point of view, this person should have every opportunity to contribute on the individual's behalf. If some choose to communicate in writing or by other means, such as e-mail, then those comments must be taken into account. If there have been any changes in organisational policies or access to resources, or changes in the circumstances of the service provider, these are also key matters and should be fed into the review for consideration.

If any conflict or difficulty arises in relation to the care plan because of feedback or observations, you must ensure that organisational procedures are followed to address the issues raised.

Supporting people to contribute

You may need to support the individual to recognise the impact of significant change and to identify the differences between important and unimportant changes. You may wish to use a prompt such as:

> Sara, your sister coming to live nearby is something which has happened to you since the last review, isn't it? Do you think things will change much for you?

> John, have you found that your new job has made much of a difference to you?

> Marvin, has having an extra afternoon at the centre made the difference you hoped for at the last review?

You may also need to support individuals to complete any paperwork that is necessary for the review or for the implementation of any revised care plan.

Care workers and other members of your team may also need support in order to contribute to the review meeting. They may feel intimidated, particularly if they are unfamiliar with speaking in front of a roomful of people.

You can encourage them to prepare for the meeting by:
- putting together a list of all the records they have kept on the individual
- informing them of their role in the meeting and preparing them for questions they may be asked
- checking they are familiar with your organisational procedures and that they understand the process.

Making decisions

Once all the information has been gathered and all contributions have been made, those taking part in the review will need to make a decision about any necessary changes to the care plan and the care package for the next period of time. Decisions should clearly be based on the monitoring of evidence and should particularly take account of contributions from the individual and his or her carers.

A review should not take a decision about changing provision with which the individual fundamentally disagrees. If the proposed changes are because of a change in the level of available resources and result in a reduction in service to the individual, it may be that such a decision is inevitable. However, it is important that the alternative which will be in place is acceptable to the individual.

If the individual is dissatisfied at the end of the review, it is important he or she is informed about the complaints procedure and the process for asking for a further review of the resources available. Full access should be ensured by offering advocacy or any other support services that may be required for individuals to take full advantage of any complaints system or further routes to changing decisions, such as approaching decision makers or accessing pressure groups.

Setting the next review date

At the end of each review it is essential that the date is set for the next review and that all the participants, particularly the individual and his or her carers, find the date acceptable, both in terms of their own availability and the length of time before the review is due to take place.

Reviews must be undertaken at least once a year and if an individual is receiving a care package under the care programme approach system through the mental health services, any admission to hospital must generate a review within a month of discharge.

Evidence indicator

Carry out an analysis of the last care plan review in which you were involved. Consider:

- the roles and responsibilities of the people involved in the review
- the quality and detail of the feedback
- whether changes were identified
- whether the review was person-centred
- how any conflict was handled
- how the review was recorded.

Keep your notes for your portfolio.

How the review process is recorded

 Keys to good practice: Recording a care package review

All reviews must be recorded in the individual's records. Confidentiality must be respected and the records must include:

✔ written reports from each care service included in the care package

✔ a record that all relevant staff have been invited to attend the review or to contribute in writing

✔ a record showing how the individual has been prepared for the review and the access he or she has to an advocate if required

✔ evidence that relevant carers and others who offer support have been invited to contribute

✔ a record of all those who attended or who contributed

✔ a careful record of any changes

✔ the revised care plan as a separate document.

Many organisations still have their own documentation (although under the single assessment process, joint records are increasingly being produced). They are likely to cover most or all of the above points.

It is important that all those who have contributed, even if they have not been present at the review, are informed of the outcome and that they know of any changes to the care plan for the individual.

Recorded reviews contribute to the overall quality of the service any organisation offers and they are likely to be included in any file audit undertaken during inspection processes. The review process, if it is well conducted, provides a vital opportunity for individuals to contribute and to make choices about the care package they receive.

Reviews that are badly prepared and carelessly undertaken rob individuals of the opportunity to take decisions which affect their lives significantly, and they also result in an ineffective use of scarce and valuable resources.

Test yourself

Mrs McPhail is a woman aged 91. She lives alone and is finding it increasingly difficult to get upstairs to the bathroom and also to bed. Fortunately her house has a downstairs toilet, but because of her difficulty in accessing the bathroom her personal hygiene has deteriorated, and she has also begun to sleep in an armchair instead of making her way upstairs to her bedroom.

1   What should happen now for Mrs McPhail?

2   Who should be involved in considering the next steps?

3   How can you make sure that Mrs McPhail is involved in the process?

4   In what ways can changes such as these be monitored?

5   Who is responsible for monitoring changes for Mrs McPhail?

HSC 328 UNIT TEST

1   How would you support an individual to identify and communicate his or her needs and preferences in relation to a care plan?

2   Why is ongoing assessment of care plans important in maintaining the quality of service provision?

3   How can individuals, their families and carers contribute to the assessment process?

4   How can you support colleagues to carry out care plan activities for which they are responsible?

5   What types of changes in an individual's needs may you notice when you are carrying out your role providing the service?

6   How can individuals with communication differences be involved in reviews?

7   What factors do you need to take into account when there is a problem about obtaining an individual's consent to a care plan?

8   What factors must the key worker take into account when balancing issues such as risk and challenge against the protection and safety of an individual?

Support individuals to access and use services and facilities

In this unit you will have the opportunity to think about how you can best support individuals to identify and communicate their needs and how you can pass information to individuals that will enable them to gain access to the most useful services and facilities. Regardless of your role and area of work, you will at some point need to provide information to those you work with or their relatives or friends. It is important that you understand how to access and update that information and how you can assist people, not only to consider services but to use them where they need support.

Information is knowledge, and it makes a huge contribution towards empowering people. Familiarity with the services and facilities that are available and accessible will provide service users with the opportunity to increase their level of independence.

What you need to learn

- How to establish the services needed
- How to obtain accurate information
- Legislation about information
- How information is stored
- Reviewing information
- How to make information accessible
- How to support people to use services
- Overcoming barriers
- Enabling people to use services and facilities
- How to evaluate services and facilities
- Methods of checking information
- How to give useful feedback on services and facilities.

What	Who	Where
Pensions/benefits	Benefits Agency, social services, Welfare Rights Centre, voluntary organisations	Welfare Rights Centre, Claimant's Union, Benefits Agency, Citizens Advice Bureau
Education	Local education office, college of further education, library	Town or county hall, telephone directory, Internet
Sports	Leisure services department, specialist voluntary organisations (e.g. National Organisation for Sport for the Disabled, International Paralympic Committee, Riding for the Disabled)	Town hall, Citizens Advice Bureau, library, Internet, Yellow Pages
Mobile library	Libraries/leisure services department	Town hall
Cinema, theatre and entertainment, clubs and pubs	Leisure services department, theatres and cinemas, local tourist office	Town hall, library, Internet, What's On guide, tourist office, local newspapers

 CASE STUDY: Finding out about needs

Vijay was a young man in his mid-twenties who used a wheelchair following a spinal injury. Vijay was provided with 24-hour care and had a team of support workers. Recently Vijay had appeared to be somewhat unhappy. He said he was bored and wanted something more exciting to do. His support worker suggested a range of options including visiting the cinema, the theatre, going to a social club or visiting an art gallery – all of which were interests of Vijay's. However, every suggestion was rejected without Vijay giving any clear reason why.

A few days later a different support worker decided to approach matters in a different way, and through questioning she established that Vijay would very much like to take up any of the suggestions made earlier, but had assumed that to do any of them he needed to take a taxi and this was something he felt unable to afford. Vijay had not liked to say that he could not afford the taxi and so had simply refused any of the suggestions.

The second support worker was able to explain to Vijay that the local authority operated a dial-a-ride service with a small bus specially adapted for wheelchairs, and that Vijay could book this service and use it for a nominal charge. There was also a taxicard scheme entitling eligible users to a certain number of taxi journeys per month at dial-a-ride prices. Vijay was delighted and began to make plans for a range of visits and activities.

1 *What was the mistake made in giving information to Vijay?*

2 *What may have happened if the second support worker had not spoken to Vijay?*

3 *What can you learn from this?*

How to obtain accurate information

No one expects you to have your head full of information to pass on to people! However, you do need to know where to find information and the best and most efficient ways of doing so. You also need to know how to keep information so that you have access to it whenever you need to use or update it.

We now live in an information society – masses of information are available on more subjects than you ever knew existed. It is easy to become confused and end up with information that will not serve a useful purpose for the individuals you work with.

Local sources of information

One of the most useful sources of information is the 'one-stop shop' approach of organisations such as the Citizens Advice Bureau. You may also find that your local Council for Voluntary Service or your local authority may have an information point; these are often located in libraries, town halls, civic centres or other easily accessible places. At these points you can usually obtain leaflets and information, and staff are available to find out more for you and to offer advice on specific areas of need. Most advice centres will find information for you if they do not have it to hand.

You may be looking for specific information in response to an individual's request or you may be generally updating your own information so that you are ready to deal promptly with any information requests. In either case, any of these facilities provide you with a very good starting point.

Many excellent sources of information are available to you locally

Special interest groups

Another excellent source of information is the range of specific interest groups such as Age Concern, the Alzheimer's Society, Mencap, Scope, and so on.

These are a wonderful source of information about facilities and services, specifically related to those with a particular condition. The contact addresses and telephone numbers for these organisations will be found at your starting point advice centre, such as the Citizens Advice Bureau or your local library or voluntary services. All of these organisations also have websites with a wealth of information and links to other websites of interest. The websites can be found by typing the name of an organisation, or of a condition such as Alzheimer's, into a search engine such as Google.

The Internet

One of the best sources of information is the Internet. To use this you will need access to a computer connected to the Internet and some skill or experience in using the various search engines in order to locate relevant websites.

Remember

When researching information on the Internet, be careful to use reliable websites such as official government sites and those of reputable organisations.

The information that you can obtain from the Internet is almost unlimited and covers every possible subject. However, you must be aware that this information is not subject to any form of verification or control, and therefore it is not always possible to confirm its accuracy. If you are finding information from the Internet to pass on to individuals, you should obtain it primarily from official websites of relevant organisations for the particular area of interest.

Other useful websites are official government sites and those of universities and research establishments. You may find that there are government reports and results of inquiries, or research findings, that are relevant to individuals with whom you work. Using the Internet can be a very quick and easy way of gaining accurate and up-to-date information, often before it has appeared in print or become readily accessible in other ways.

Encouraging individuals to use the Internet

For many individuals, accessing information for themselves over the Internet can be useful and can motivate them to explore the huge potential of the World Wide Web. This can provide many people with a new hobby, as can be seen from the massive interest in 'Silver Surfers' groups being run around the country by Age Concern. The take-up of these classes for older people has been huge, and many people now have the skills to access information for themselves. Beware of assuming that anyone over the age of 60 knows nothing about 'surfing the Net' – you may be surprised to find that they are much more able than you are!

The Internet can also provide many people with the opportunity to network with others who have similar interests and issues. This can help to broaden the social contacts of individuals who may otherwise find themselves with limited opportunities for such contact. However, you should make sure individuals are well aware of the basic precautions that should be taken when using the Internet in this way:

- remember that because of free and unrestricted access to the Internet, not every message is genuine and truthful
- never give out your address, telephone number or any financial information
- if you arrange to meet someone you have come into contact with via the Internet, meet in a public place and do not go alone.

There are also many useful opportunities for education and training via online learning materials. This can make learning more accessible and may offer the chance for new knowledge and understanding which may not be available through traditional teaching approaches.

There are increasing opportunities for people to access the Internet even if they do not have their own computers. Cyber cafés and many libraries, local town halls, colleges and universities have facilities for public access to the Internet, usually for a small fee. You might encourage people to take advantage of these if appropriate. As always, the best approach is to support individuals to be self-managing and to find out information for themselves.

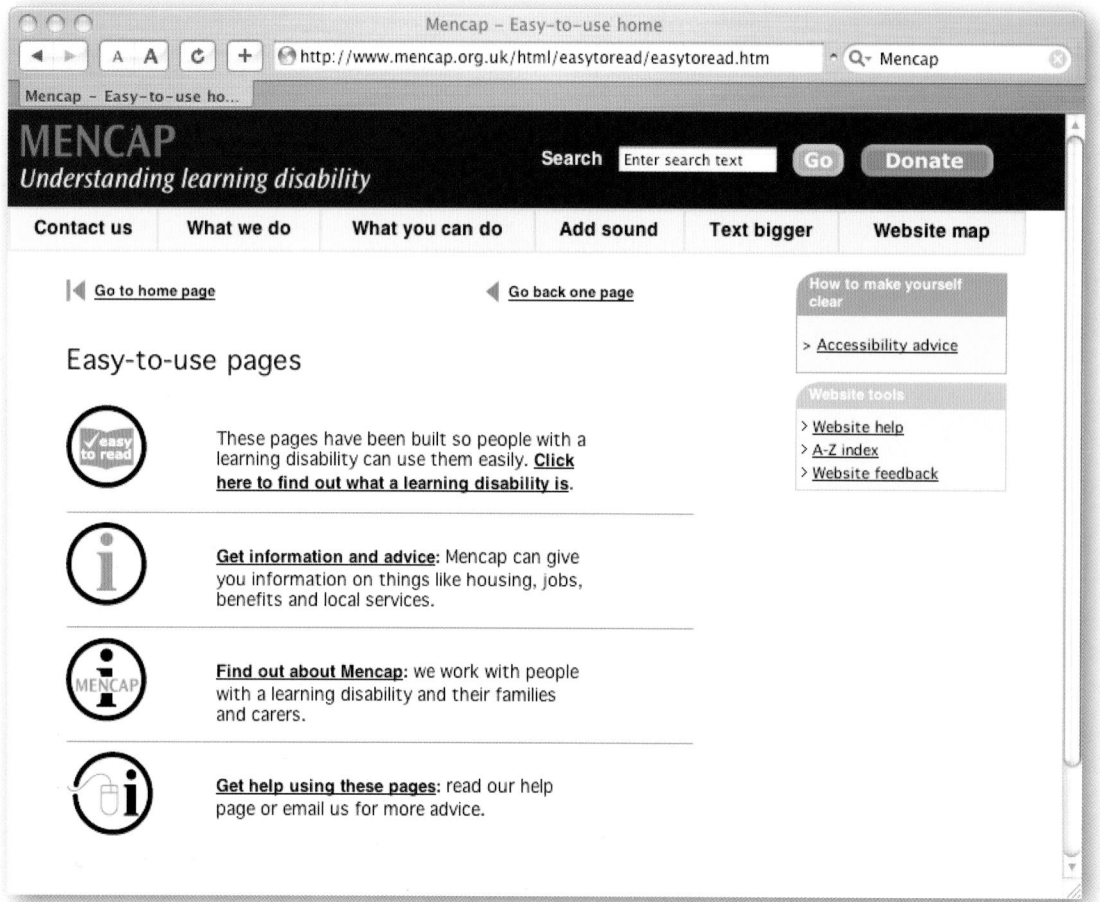

Mencap's website is an excellent source of easy-to-access information

clearly understood and found well in advance, is far more likely to be able to challenge and overcome difficulties than someone who feels uncertain because of a lack of information, and is unprepared for any difficulties.

Barriers to access tend to fall into three categories: environmental, communication, and psychological. Environmental barriers are the most common.

Environmental barriers	• lack of disabled toilet facilities • high-risk or threatening location, e.g. near a busy pub or parade of shops which is a known hang-out for gangs of young men • narrow doorways • no ramps • no lifts • lack of transport or lack of access by transport • lack of wheelchair access
Communication barriers	• lack of loop system • poor quality communication skills in staff at the facility, e.g. an unhelpful or obstructive receptionist • lack of translators or interpreters • lack of information or publicity about the service or facility • lack of information in an appropriate language or format
Psychological barriers	• unfamiliarity • lack of confidence • fear or anxiety • concern at loss of independence • unwillingness to accept help

How to challenge and overcome barriers

Start by checking that all possible information is available about the facilities and services, the challenges and the alternatives. Work alongside an individual to help plan ways to challenge and overcome any discrimination and barriers. For example, you may need to support someone to search out alternative facilities if the ones originally found do not have wheelchair access.

If the local theatre does not have wheelchair access, encourage the individual to make arrangements to travel to one that does. Of course, you could also encourage the individual to raise the issue with the local theatre and point out to them that they are in breach of the Disability Discrimination Act.

If there are problems finding suitable transport, it will be necessary to find out about transport with provision for wheelchairs, by checking local taxi or public transport facilities which have the necessary adaptations. Most train companies have support services for people with disabilities, such as ramps and a porter service to enable people to get on and off trains. However, many trains that do provide porterage and ramps do not have readily accessible toilets for disabled people.

Any particular arrangements with a facility to provide access must be agreed with the individual concerned. If a person who uses a wheelchair has to make an important visit to a particular location which cannot be changed and there is no wheelchair access through the main entrance, it may be suggested that the individual use a back entrance or goods entrance and the goods lift. You should always check with the individual before agreeing to this type of arrangement, as not everyone is prepared to access a building through a goods entrance. Many disabled people take the view that they should have the right to access buildings in the same way as everyone else. In such a case, you may need to support the individual in arranging for the visit to take place at a different location. It is essential you never compromise the right of an individual to choose his or her own means of access and to set boundaries as to what is acceptable in terms of personal space and dignity.

An individual has the right to set boundaries as to what is acceptable in terms of dignity

Evidence indicator

Choose three different types of facility that people may wish to access in your locality. They should each be located in a different part of your area. For each, list the potential barriers to access and the ways in which you would begin to tackle the barriers. Keep your notes for your portfolio.

Enabling people to use services and facilities

The level of support that you need to provide to an individual will vary depending on the circumstances. Your support can range from handing someone an information leaflet to making all the arrangements to use a service and accompanying him or her to use it. Between these extremes are a wide range of alternatives. Some people may simply need you to make the initial contact for them. Others may need you to accompany them on a first visit to a new facility or to meet a new group of people, and then to gradually withdraw as they grow in confidence in using the service. On other occasions your role may be to enlist the support of other people who are better qualified, more experienced or who have the resources or time to provide a better service for the individual.

It is important you encourage people to dispense with your support as soon as they feel able to manage independently. You should do this when you notice them becoming more confident in using the facility or service. Do it by gradually and appropriately reducing the level of support.

For example, you may have accompanied someone on a first visit to a Welfare Rights Advice Centre. The individual needed you because he or she was unfamiliar with the service and did not understand the benefit system enough to be able to explain the information required. However, as the visits continue and the work of the Welfare Rights Advice Centre is under way, you may be able to withdraw from accompanying the individual as he or she becomes more familiar with the workers in the centre. Your involvement may then be limited to driving the individual to the centre, or holding a support session on his or her return.

It may take people a while to adjust with confidence to new social situations. For example, if someone has been supported by you to find out about and then visit a new day centre or social club, it may take a few visits before he or she is confident enough to go alone. As always your role is to do the minimum and to allow individuals the maximum opportunity to make their own lives and to be as independent as possible.

Test yourself

1   Give three points to consider when providing information about services and facilities.

2   Name three barriers to accessing and using services and facilities.

3   How could those barriers be overcome?

4   Describe an occasion when you provided support to an individual using services or facilities. Evaluate how successful this was for the individual concerned.

HSC 330c Enable individuals to evaluate services and facilities used

How to evaluate services and facilities

Evaluation is often thought to be a difficult and complex process, but in fact it is straightforward. The process of evaluating an event or experience is extremely useful because it allows you to find out:

- what worked well
- what worked badly or didn't work at all
- what was wrong and can be fixed
- what was wrong and can't be fixed
- what you would do/use again
- what you would not do/use again
- what was better than you expected
- what was worse than you expected
- what needs to be changed
- what should stay the same
- what you need to do next time.

The simplest way to find out about any of the items on this list is to ask for feedback. In the case of a service, a product or a facility, all those involved in providing, recommending or using it need to know whether it is working well.

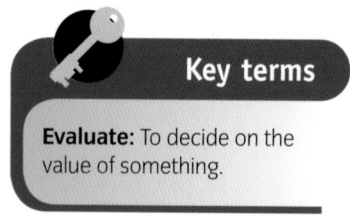

Key terms

Evaluate: To decide on the value of something.

CASE STUDY: Compiling a directory

Students at a local college were studying for a health and social care qualification. For one of their assignments they were asked to produce a directory of information about entertainment and leisure facilities in the local area. When they had completed the project, the students decided to present the finished directory to the supported living unit at 24 The Avenue. This unit provides supported living for eight people with a disability, some of whom have complex needs.

The directory was printed out and stapled to form a booklet. The work had been done very neatly and each facility was identified in bold lettering, followed by a short description of the facilities, like this:

> **Royal Theatre**
> Plays, concerts and shows. Weekly programme of events. Seats 500. Tickets through box office 10.00hrs–20.00hrs 0123 45678. Café available 11.00hrs–18.00hrs. Facilities DT, WA, L, B, H (see key on p. 5)

A few weeks later, staff noticed that the directory was lying in the lounge and no one seemed to have used it.

1 *What do you think may be the reason why the directory was not used?*

2 *How could the directory be improved?*

3 *What sort of information should be in it?*

4 *How should it be presented?*

5 *What should the residents and staff of the unit do now?*

Methods of checking information

The basic requirement for any sort of information is that it should be:

- accurate
- relevant
- up to date
- easy to understand
- accessible to everyone
- within the law.

You need to encourage individuals to check that information is accurate and relevant for their purposes. It also helps if information is interesting!

People who provide information need to know whether it is all of those things, so feedback is essential. You should encourage and support people in providing feedback about information they have accessed or tried to access.

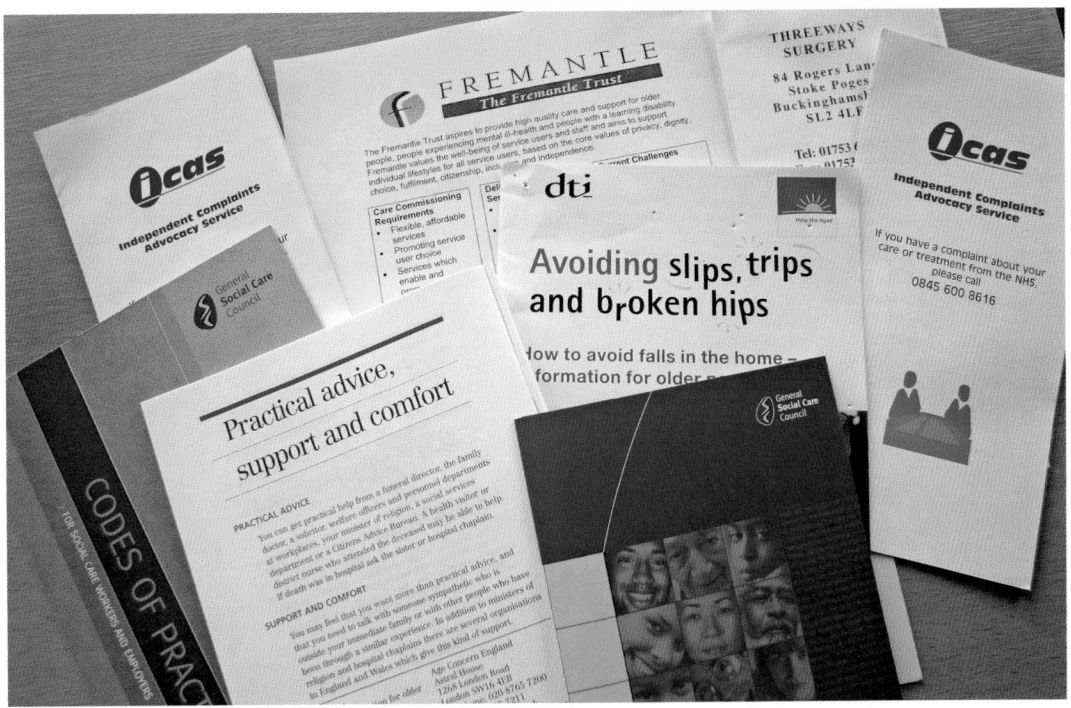

Information needs to be accurate, relevant and accessible

If you have tried to obtain information about welfare rights and it was not available in large print, this fact can be fed back to the co-ordinator of the Welfare Rights Centre. However, it will be important that you encourage the individual concerned to check that information has improved, otherwise the feedback will have been wasted.

In the case of commercial businesses, shops, supermarkets, cinemas, entertainment centres or theatres, feedback should be given to the manager on site. Some businesses may be part of a national or international chain and information may be handled centrally. Where this is the case, you should encourage and support people to seek out those who have responsibility for the information policy of the company and make sure they receive the feedback.

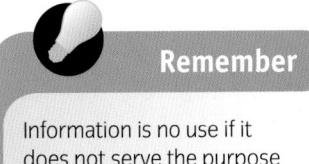

Remember

Information is no use if it does not serve the purpose for which it was needed!

How to give useful feedback on services and facilities

You will need to agree the methods and timescales you will use with an individual and his or her carers for evaluating how the use of services or facilities has contributed to his or her well-being. People's needs do not remain the same, so services and facilities that appeared to meet an individual's needs at one time may no longer be appropriate after quite a short period of time. Regular review and feedback will therefore be needed. Feedback should identify:

- the services and facilities the individual has selected and used
- any discrimination or exclusion that the individual has experienced
- which services and facilities have been beneficial to the individual's well-being
- which services and facilities have been less helpful
- the reasons for the helpfulness or lack of helpfulness in each case.

As a care professional you know that receiving feedback is not always easy and that criticism can sometimes make you feel resentful. So you should encourage individuals offering feedback to ensure they make positive suggestions alongside any complaints they may have. No one likes receiving a long list of complaints and criticism, even if it is well deserved. People are much more receptive to feedback if it is accompanied by useful suggestions about how matters could be improved. This will help them to improve the quality of the services they provide, and should mean that others will not experience the same problems in the future.

Evidence indicator

Explain the process of evaluating services and facilities used in your workplace. Check who is responsible for evaluating and how they undertake the task. Ask where the resulting information is kept and how its usefulness is checked. Keep your notes for your portfolio.

Identifying and implementing necessary changes

Constructive feedback involves identifying the changes necessary to improve the outcomes for individuals using services and facilities. Your role in supporting this process may include collating information, records and reports connected with the evaluation. You must follow organisational procedures and remember the rules of confidentiality when you are working with such information.

Evaluation is of no use unless it results in the appropriate changes being made. You will need to work with the individuals and key people involved to achieve the changes that have been identified as being necessary for the improvement of services and facilities. You will also need to support them in challenging any discrimination or exclusion they have experienced.

However, as with the selection of services, it will be important that you do not misuse your position of trust with the individual in order to influence the feedback he or she gives so that it reflects *your* opinion of services and facilities. There will be channels through which you can communicate your own experiences and opinions, and these will have their own value; but you must ensure they are kept clearly separate from the feedback given by the individual himself or herself.

Test yourself

1   How could you offer support to individuals in evaluating the services and facilities they use?

2   Why should individuals be encouraged to offer constructive suggestions alongside any criticisms?

3   What procedures are in place to ensure feedback is acted upon in your workplace?

4   Why is it important that feedback is seen to be taken seriously and acted upon?

HSC 330 UNIT TEST

1   What are the main sources of information about services and facilities?

2   How would you go about collecting and storing a general information bank?

3   What are the key factors to take into account when providing people with information about services and facilities?

4   What are the potential pitfalls in the way that facilities and services are provided?

5   What are the effective ways of encouraging people to access and use services and facilities?

6   Name four potential barriers to accessing services and facilities.

7   How could these barriers be overcome?

8   Explain the importance of supporting individuals to evaluate services and facilities they have used.

Contribute to the prevention and management of abusive and aggressive behaviour

When people need care, difficulties and conflicts can arise that put individuals, their carers and those around them under great stress. If these situations are not dealt with constructively, aggressive and abusive behaviour can result. In other cases, the condition of individuals causes them to become frustrated and to lose the ability to control their reactions, or to consider the consequences of their behaviour. They can then become verbally or physically aggressive to those around them.

It is a vital part of your work that you contribute to the prevention and management of any abusive and aggressive behaviour. It is not always preventable, so when it occurs you need to be able to deal with it appropriately. You also need to help in the review of such incidents according to the policies of your workplace and in a way that satisfies legal requirements.

This unit does not address systematic abuse. It is concerned with incidents of verbal or non-verbal behaviour which is abusive and/or aggressive. But this is as difficult an area to deal with as the prevention of systematic abuse and neglect, discussed in Unit HSC 35, and you will need to be clear about your role and learn how to manage the feelings aroused by such incidents.

What you need to learn

- Ways of communicating appropriately
- Knowing yourself and your own behaviour
- How to listen
- How to maintain an emotionally safe atmosphere
- Causes of abusive or aggressive behaviour
- How to minimise the risk of aggression or abuse
- Behaviour that is unacceptable
- How to respond to unacceptable behaviour
- Physical restraint issues
- Recording an incident
- How dealing with abuse or aggression can affect you
- Encouraging those involved to contribute to a review.

HSC 336a Contribute to preventing abusive and aggressive behaviour

Good communication is vital in preventing the conflicts and frustrations that can lead to abusive or aggressive behaviour.

People communicate differently, and the varieties in communication styles can result from differences in culture and background. Culture is about more than the language people speak – it is about the way that they live, think and relate to each other.

Ways of communicating appropriately

You need to communicate with others in ways which:

- are appropriate for them
- encourage open exchanges of views and information
- minimise constraints to communication
- are free from discrimination and oppression
- acknowledge and support the rights of everyone involved.

In order for you to work as an effective communicator, you must know how to deal with people in a way which takes account of their individuality. When time is short and demands are high, it is often easier to treat everyone in a group in the same way, to make plans for a whole group of people or to assume that what is good for one person will be good for all. Learning how to avoid this is an important part of your job.

Each person you work with is an individual – completely different and unique. This may sound obvious but it is so important that it is worth repeating. Making judgements about people which are based not on knowledge and understanding of that person but on generally accepted stereotypes, often with little truth behind them, is a recipe for conflict.

Working in caring is not only about having good working relationships with colleagues, although good teamwork is essential; it is also about the relationships you make with the individuals you are caring for, and it is about understanding other relationships they have, with their friends and relatives.

Avoiding stereotypes

One of the most effective ways you have of helping people is by recognising them as individuals. As discussed in Unit HSC 35, it is vital never to make assumptions about people in groups.

Think about the number of ways in which people can be identified – they can be described by age, gender, eye colour, place of residence, job, special interests, and any number of personal characteristics. This will remind you of the number of different aspects there are to any one individual.

The problem with 'labelling' people by placing them in particular groups for particular purposes is that it is very rarely accurate. It may be very convenient when planning care to decide that 'all individuals will want ...' or 'this age group will benefit from ...', but the number of individuals contained within any group means that any planning that starts with a generalisation is doomed to be unsatisfactory.

Remember that people are different, enjoy different activities and have different needs

Active knowledge

Think of a way to describe yourself, starting with the most general – 'I am a woman' or 'I am a man'. So are other people, so that does not describe you. 'I have brown hair' – so do a great many others. Continue thinking of ways to describe yourself, getting closer all the time to finding a description that is unique to you (one that describes you, and no one else). Each time you think of another way to describe yourself, it will eliminate more and more people from the group, until finally you may (depending on how well you know yourself) come up with a description which applies to no one else but you.

Each time you are tempted to treat people as one of a group, remember how long this task took and how many descriptions you listed before you found a unique reference to you. Remember that everyone you deal with is unique – an individual.

It will be important to be aware of the risk of stereotyped thinking when you are assessing the degree of risk involved in working with someone who is distressed. Stereotyping might result in dangerous assumptions such as 'only men are violent, so I need not worry about the reaction of this woman' or 'I can relax with this person because he is like me – so nothing can go wrong'.

Equally, stereotyping may result in discriminatory assumptions such as 'I cannot possibly work on my own with people who have dementia in case they become violent'. The stereotype this reflects is the belief that all people with a mental health problem are potentially violent. The stereotype behind the judgement that 'I may be at risk if I work with people from a different ethnic group' is that people who are different from you are dangerous!

It is always important to check your thinking for assumptions and stereotypes – unless you become good at this you may expose yourself to risk and expose service users to discrimination.

Encouraging an open exchange of views

Valuing people as individuals means having respect for all of the people you deal with. Respect is usually something that develops as you form relationships. When you provide care for someone, you will get to know and talk to him or her, and a relationship will grow. This is not easy with all individuals you care for. When there appears to be no two-way communication, you may find that forming a relationship is difficult.

Remember

- Everyone has the right to make choices.
- All people are different.

If you accept these points, you will never be guilty of making generalisations or making prejudiced judgements about people again.

Keys to good practice: Respecting individuals

✓ Make sure that any service you provide for someone is with his or her agreement. People have a right to choose the care they receive and the way in which they receive it.

✓ Set a good example by being open to the views expressed by others. Encourage people to listen to and respect each other's views.

Of course, people cannot suddenly stop doing and thinking things which they have been doing and thinking all their lives, and begin to agree with each other on every point; but they can be encouraged to develop an awareness of everyone's right to a different point of view.

Once you realise how your own background and beliefs alter the way you think about people, you can begin to recognise the differences and see the value of other cultures and beliefs. It is inevitable that, by thinking carefully about what has influenced you, you will also consider what has influenced others with whom you come into contact.

You need to talk to people, whether they are colleagues or service users, about aspects of their culture or lifestyle you do not understand. As a care professional, it is your responsibility to make sure that you have considered the culture, beliefs and lifestyle of someone for whom you are providing care. It is not acceptable to expect that they will adapt to your set of cultural beliefs and expectations.

If you work to create the kind of environment in which everyone's contribution is valued, and where meaningful interactions can take place between people with very different needs or backgrounds, you will be making an enormous contribution to preventing inappropriate behaviour. The diversity of the human race is what makes living in our society such a rich and varied experience. If you welcome this diversity, and encourage others to do so rather than resist, condemn or belittle the things they do not understand, the relationships among colleagues and service users will be much more rewarding and the quality of your care practice will be greatly improved.

Knowing yourself and your own behaviour

It is vital, if you are to help people to live and work together effectively, that you understand how you affect any situation. Human beings do not react in the same way to everyone. You have doubtless had the experience of meeting people who make you feel relaxed and at ease – you find it easy to talk to them and feel as if you had known them for a long time. Equally, there are other people who seem much harder to talk to – in their presence you feel nervous, or unsure; you can't think of anything to say and feel generally uncomfortable. You are still the same person, but you have reacted in a totally different way to different people.

To be a good practitioner in caring, you have to learn to understand how people react to *you* and the way in which your own beliefs, background and prejudices will influence the outcome of an interaction with another person.

It is essential that you understand about interaction between people if you are working in caring. It is not always easy to understand how it works. It may help if you think about dealing with other people as being like looking in different fairground mirrors. All of the reflections look different – some are short and fat, some long and thin, some are wavy and curved; it all depends on the mirror. You are still the same, but the mirror makes everything appear different. In the same way, you will interact differently depending on the person you are talking to.

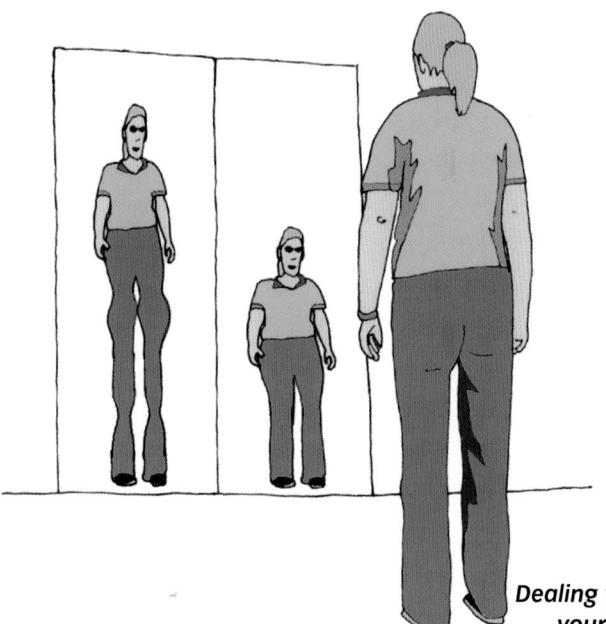

Dealing with different people is like seeing yourself in different fairground mirrors

Remember

- Stereotypes can influence how you think about someone.
- Don't rush to make judgements about people.
- Everyone is entitled to his or her own beliefs and culture. If you don't know about someone's way of life – ask.

Evidence indicator

Try this for yourself at work. Pick two different people and tell them both the same piece of information. For example, you could explain why a particular individual needs a change in the plan of care, or describe where the new delivery of equipment has been stored – in fact, anything at all.

Note down how you carried out the task with each person and how you felt. Make sure you note the differences in your behaviour and feelings. Try to work out how, and why, each of them made you feel different. Keep your notes for your portfolio.

Learning about yourself is not an easy task. Often you never take the time to examine your own behaviour in depth. It can be a shock when someone points out something you are doing, or a way you have of behaving, which you had not realised.

If you intend to be effective as a carer, you will need to spend some time looking at your own behaviour, and try to look in the mirror of other people's reactions.

Keys to good practice: Examining your own behaviour

✓ **Are your interactions sometimes unsuccessful?** If you are talking to someone and he or she suddenly seems to close down the conversation, or appear frustrated, try to think back to the point at which the atmosphere changed. Be honest with yourself. Did you react to something he or she said? Did you say something that was a little thoughtless? Did you laugh in a way that could have been interpreted as unkind? Or did he or she begin to back away when you looked at your watch, or spoke briefly to someone else who wanted your attention?

✓ **Do some individuals seem to find it easier to talk to you than others?** Do you find it easier to talk to some individuals than others? Of course, there are bound to be some people you like more than others, but when you are working as a professional carer it is not enough just to acknowledge that. You have to think about the reasons in order to make sure that it does not result in individuals being treated differently.

✓ **Only you can work at examining your own behaviour.** If you have a manager or colleague to work with you, that is a great help, but essentially no one can do it for you. You will need to be able to consider a series of questions: Which people do you find it hard to deal with? Can you work better with women than men? Do you find it hard to talk to young people? or to older people? or to people of a particular social class? or to people of particular races? or to anyone with a different accent?

✓ **Do you find that you have less patience with some people?** Can you identify which people? Is there a pattern? You may not always like the answers you come up with, but until you can work out how you behave towards others and why, you will never be able to make any adjustments to your responses.

Continued

Remember

You can change the way you behave by reflecting on your own behaviour, deciding what you need to change and practising new approaches until they become natural to you.

Keys to good practice: Examining your own behaviour

✓ **Look at your own culture and beliefs.** You may, for example, have grown up surrounded by people who believed that it was unthinkable to owe a penny to anyone, so you may find it difficult to offer empathy and support to someone who is desperate because he or she is deeply in debt. If you have lived in a culture which holds older family members in high regard and gives them great respect, you may find it hard to relate to the family of an older person if they hardly ever visit and do not appear interested in his or her welfare. Nevertheless, in your role as a carer you have to be aware of how your own background may influence you and to ensure that you include that factor in the analysis of any situation.

✓ **Don't be too hard on yourself.** If you acknowledge your own prejudices you will be more than halfway towards overcoming them. Just being able to understand why you behave in the way you do is more than most people achieve in a lifetime! So don't worry if it takes a while before you feel that you are really thinking effectively about what you do and how you affect others. Knowing how people respond to you and making allowances for that will, eventually, become second nature.

How to listen

The key areas of listening and talking are where people interact meaningfully. You may think that this comes naturally to most people, but everyone can learn some basic skills which will improve their communication significantly.

Active listening

Active listening is about doing much more than simply hearing the words which an individual is speaking. It includes encouraging someone to talk to you, letting him or her know that you are interested, concerned and supportive, and allowing him or her the space, time and attention to express feelings and concerns in a calm manner.

Remember

- To hear what someone is really telling you, you have to be a good listener.

- To help someone understand what you are saying and to tell you what he or she wants to say, you have to be a good communicator.

recognising where it can happen. If a known trigger to unacceptable behaviour occurs, you may be able to act quickly to divert an individual to other activities, or take other preventive action. When risk situations occur in the community, you may be in a position to intervene directly or to report to your supervisor and offer suggestions about ways to reduce risks.

Try to ensure that people in potentially difficult situations are offered as much support as possible. However difficult the circumstances, a person is less likely to resort to aggression or abuse if he or she feels supported, acknowledged and appreciated. Showing sympathy and understanding for a person's situation can often defuse potential explosions. A care worker could express this by saying, for example, 'It must be so hard caring for your mother. The demands she makes are so difficult. I think you are doing a wonderful job.' Such comments can often help someone to feel that he or she is understood and that there are people who are able and willing to support him or her.

Keys to good practice: Minimising risks

✓ Always prevent a difficult situation from arising if you can. If you know, for example, that two people regularly disagree violently about everything from politics to whether or not it is raining, try to arrange that they are involved in separate activities and, if possible, have seats in separate lounges! Alternatively, you may decide to deal with the situation by talking to them both, and offering to help them resolve their disagreements.

✓ Only intervene directly if there is an immediate risk. You will need to use your communication skills to ensure that you handle the situation in a way that does not make things worse and will ensure that you protect the person at risk. Ask for support if necessary.

✓ If there is no immediate risk, report the incident and get assistance as soon as possible.

Providing support

Some situations require much more than words of support, and giving practical, physical support to an individual, a carer or a family may help to reduce the risk of aggression or abuse.

While your support is vital in preventing a potential aggressor from behaving unacceptably, you must also protect potential victims of such behaviour. When resources are provided within the community rather than at home, this also offers a chance to observe someone who is thought to be at risk. Day centres, training centres, schools, after-school clubs and youth centres also provide an opportunity for people to talk to staff and to feel that they are in a supportive environment where they can talk about any problems and they will be listened to and helped.

Remember

- Preventing abusive or aggressive behaviour is better than having to deal with it.

- Support may make all the difference to a person under stress.

- Only intervene directly if there is an immediate risk.

- Act assertively to stop any aggressive or abusive behaviour.

HSC 336b Deal with incidents of abusive and aggressive behaviour

Behaviour that is unacceptable

All abusive and aggressive behaviour is unacceptable. However, you may come across other kinds of behaviour which you may not be able to define directly as abusive, but which are close to it or could lead to such behaviour if not dealt with.

People have a right to express their views in an assertive way; in fact one could say it is a duty to act assertively to protect one's own or someone else's rights. The difference between assertive and aggressive behaviour is that the latter fails to treat other people with respect and infringes their rights. Generally, you can define behaviour as unacceptable if:

- it does not take into account the needs or views of others
- people are afraid or intimidated
- people are undermined or made to feel guilty
- the behaviour is likely to cause distress or unhappiness to others.

Examples of unacceptable behaviour include:
- threatening violence
- subjecting someone to unwelcome sexual attention
- seriously disturbing others, for example by shouting or playing loud music in a quiet area, or late at night
- verbal abuse, racist or sexist taunts
- spreading malicious gossip about someone
- attempting to isolate someone.

All of these types of behaviour are oppressive to others and need to be challenged. You can probably think of many other situations in your own workplace which have caused unhappiness. You may have had to deal with difficult situations, or have seen others deal with them, or perhaps you have wished that you had done something to challenge unacceptable behaviour.

How to respond to unacceptable behaviour

What happens when people become aggressive?

Anger is a powerful emotion and it often seems as if people suddenly lose their temper without a reason. A service user might suddenly start shouting or making abusive comments. But this service user might have felt stressed long before the outburst of anger. Frustration and tension can grow as an individual loses control over his or her emotions and circumstances.

Triggers

As tension mounts it may take only a single remark or a small thing going wrong to push someone into an angry outburst. People who feel stressed may only need a minor incident to act as a trigger to set off an explosion of the anger that has built up inside them.

After an explosion of anger, stressed people can still feel tense. Very often they may feel that it is someone else's fault that they have been made to feel so angry. Anger can flare up again if the person is not given respect and encouraged to become calm. As time passes, tension may reduce as stress and levels of emotional arousal decrease.

Not all angry outbursts follow this pattern. Some people learn to use aggression to get their way, and some people can switch aggressive emotions on and off as they wish. Being angry can sometimes be a reaction that a person has chosen. But it is wrong to assume that most aggression and anger are deliberate; a great deal of aggression experienced by care workers is an emotional response to frustration or distress.

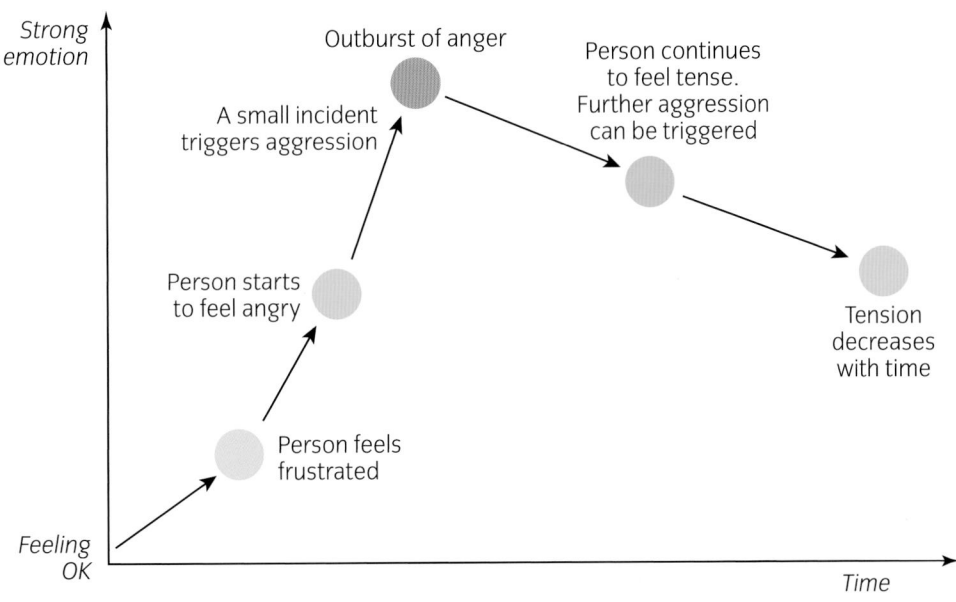

Stages in the development of aggression

The desire to fight or run

When people are aggressive or abusive they may make care workers feel threatened. The simple in-built emotional response to a threat is to want to run or fight. An unskilled response to aggression is to be aggressive in return. This will almost certainly escalate into a conflict situation, which is unlikely to have a positive outcome.

For example, imagine that an immobile resident in a care home has asked for assistance to get up but has been kept waiting. He or she may react aggressively with accusations such as: 'You don't care about me – you're too lazy to do your job properly', and so on. An unskilled response to this abuse might be to shout back at the resident, returning the abuse with statements such as 'You're not the only person here you know! I've only got one pair of hands' and so on. The problem with responding to aggression by being aggressive is that one or both people have to lose. The key purpose of care is to protect vulnerable people and meet social and self-esteem needs as well as basic physical needs. If a care worker is successful in being more aggressive than the service user, this is likely to increase the service user's sense of being out of control, lower his or her self-esteem and create increased helplessness in the individual. Depressed or withdrawn people may seem easier to manage than aggressive ones, but turning an aggressive person into a depressed person can never be acceptable.

Even in mildly aggressive encounters, one or both people are likely to feel resentment towards each other following the incident. You are unlikely to have job satisfaction if you develop resentment towards the people you work with.

There is of course, no guarantee that the care worker will be the winner if a conflict situation arises. Some members of the public can become physically violent and cause physical as well as emotional injury to staff. Other members of the public may make successful formal complaints if they have received abuse. The professional, skilled response is to stay calm, be assertive rather than aggressive, try to calm the other person, and resolve the situation without creating resentment. Of course, it is much easier to describe this formula than it is to implement it in practice.

Staying in control of your own emotions

We are all pre-programmed to either run away from or fight anyone who threatens us. Learning to be assertive and to take control of our instincts to run or to fight is a difficult task, but many people do learn to control their emotions. It is possible to stay in control and not allow the desire to run or fight to become overpowering.

We have two systems that guide our reactions. We can think and reason using the outer part of the brain, called the cortex, and we can react to experiences with emotion – a system built into our mid-brain. Emotion is designed to enable us to respond rapidly if we are threatened. If you switched on the

If there is a reason why writing a report is not possible, then you should record your evidence on audio tape. It is not acceptable to pass on the information verbally – there must be a record that can be referred to. Your evidence may be needed by the social workers and police officers who will investigate the situation. It may be useful for a doctor who will conduct an examination, or it may be needed for a case conference or for court proceedings.

If you have witnessed, or intervened in, an act of aggression which may constitute a criminal offence, you must *not* remove any possible evidence until the police have examined the scene. If there are injuries, or the possibility of physical evidence, a medical examination must be arranged. If an adult has been affected, he or she must consent to an examination before one can be carried out. In the case of a child, the parents must consent, unless they are the suspected abusers.

Test yourself

1 List the important factors in resolving conflicts and disagreements.

2 What is the difference between being assertive and being aggressive?

3 List some examples of unacceptable behaviour that may occur, or have occurred, in your workplace and the steps for dealing with them.

4 What should you do if faced with a potentially violent situation?

HSC 336c Contribute to reviewing incidents of abusive and aggressive behaviour

How dealing with abuse or aggression can affect you

Being involved in an incident of violence or aggression can be very distressing and you should ask for support from your supervisor if you find that you are affected by an incident you have witnessed or been involved in.

Do not underestimate how upsetting it can be to deal with someone who is displaying powerful emotions. Feeling concerned, upset or even angry after a particularly difficult experience with a service user is perfectly normal. The fact that you continue to have an emotional response after a situation is over is in no way a reflection on the quality of your work or your ability as a care worker.

After dealing with any difficult or emotional situation most people are likely to continue to think about it for some time. One of the best ways to deal with this is to discuss it with your line manager or supervisor; or you could talk to a close friend or relative, always ensuring that you never compromise an individual's right to confidentiality. If you find after a period of time that you are unable to put a particular incident out of your mind or you feel that it is interfering with your work, there are other sources of help available to you, both within your workplace and outside it. Talk to your line manager or supervisor to ensure that you have access to any help you need.

Abuse and aggression will always be distressing for the person who deals with them. But if you are able to develop your skills and knowledge so that you can identify the causes of unacceptable behaviour, contribute towards reducing it and offer effective help and support to individuals, then you are making a useful contribution to the provision of quality care. The best way to channel your thoughts and feelings following an incident will be to make clear and constructive contributions to team discussions, and to undertake a careful review.

Evidence indicator

Ask an experienced colleague about the effects that dealing with difficult incidents have had on his or her working practices. Find out about the support available in your workplace following such incidents. Make notes on your findings for your portfolio.

Encouraging those involved to contribute to a review

There needs to be a process of review following an incident of abusive and aggressive behaviour to identify any action that needs to be taken, and for lessons to be learned so that such situations can be avoided in the future. You will need to offer time, space and support so that everyone involved can express their feelings and examine their behaviour.

The review should explore constructively the reasons for, and consequences of, the incident. You may need to offer support to individuals before, during or after their contribution to the review. The support you give can range from straightforward reassurance and information to relieve anxiety and apprehension about the process, to using basic counselling skills to resolve some of the issues and concerns which have resulted from the incident.

Remember

Those affected by an incident may include people who were not present, such as relatives, friends or carers of the individuals involved. They should be invited to contribute to the review.

Keys to good practice: Encouraging individuals to speak about an incident

✓ Follow the principles of good communication. Remember to talk to the individual in an appropriate environment where he or she can feel relaxed and secure.

✓ Remember that you are doing the listening, not the talking.

✓ Listen actively to what the individual tells you and prompt him or her by nodding and using encouraging words.

✓ You may need to repeat back what the individual tells you to check that you have understood and to show that you are listening well.

✓ Avoid giving direct advice if possible, but try to encourage the individual to understand for himself or herself what has happened and to look at options for the future.

If you find yourself having to offer extensive support, you should talk to your supervisor or line manager for advice or guidance. In many cases it may be necessary to make referrals to appropriate professionals for specialist help to be provided.

Self-confidence and self-esteem

Being involved in an abusive or aggressive incident can be a huge blow to someone's self-confidence and self-esteem, and low levels of these may have contributed to the fact that the incident arose in the first place. If someone is not very confident or does not have a high opinion of himself or herself, you will need to offer extra support in order for him or her to contribute to a review.

Being the victim of abuse or aggression often creates a major threat to self-esteem. For many people, being shouted at or being pushed, for example, will have little impact on their physical well-being. However, being subject to abuse can be a threat to your dignity. Being disrespected (or 'dissed' in teenage slang) can damage your emotional well-being. When people have been assaulted, the degree of physical injury may sometimes be less damaging than the emotional damage to their self-confidence and self-esteem.

Many service users in care are vulnerable people; they come into care because of a loss of health, the loss of a partner, or the loss of physical, sensory or mental abilities. Many people in care may already have low self-esteem or feel vulnerable because of their situation. Becoming the victim of abuse or aggression provides an additional threat to self-esteem.

One of the most straightforward defences that people use when their self-esteem is threatened is to withdraw from, or deny the significance of what has happened. You may find that service users do not wish to talk about an event that has damaged their self-esteem.

Counselling

In some situations people who have been victims of abuse or assault may need the support of a professional counsellor in order to assist them to make sense of events and to rebuild their self-confidence and self-esteem. It is likely that your organisation will have a procedure for contacting counselling services where staff or service users need such support.

Sometimes, skilled active listening may be enough to help a person make sense of what happened and re-establish self-esteem and confidence. It may be that by offering to talk an issue through you will be able to support a person to report or review an incident.

If you find that you are unsure about the best ways to meet the needs of particular individuals, you should discuss this with your supervisor, who will be able to give you advice based on knowledge of the individual concerned and the local facilities available.

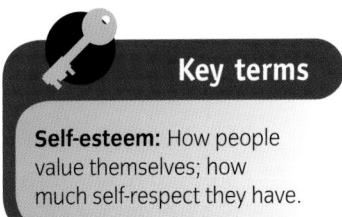

Key terms

Self-esteem: How people value themselves; how much self-respect they have.

Exploring the reasons for the behaviour

An individual may find it difficult to accept and describe the feelings of fear, frustration or anger that caused him or her to behave aggressively. Because of people's beliefs, values and culture they may not find it easy to understand or to express in a constructive way how they feel. It is important to create as many opportunities as possible for people to express their feelings openly, and the review of the incident should be conducted in such a way that people feel supported in doing this.

The stressful or angry feelings that led to the behaviour could have many causes, but the individual can be supported in finding constructive ways of coping with stress or managing anger, such as:

- talking things over with a carer, friend, relative or counsellor
- doing something to take his or her mind off the problem, if only temporarily
- using relaxation techniques such as controlled breathing, which can be taught
- undertaking physical activity such as walking, gardening or simple exercises, if possible.

Remember

Be sure that, following the review and all discussions of the incident, you complete accurate records about decisions taken and actions that are recommended for the future, and that you store your records according to workplace requirements.

Managing your own feelings

Aggression can create a high level of threat to your own self-esteem as well as a threat to your physical well-being. Even verbal abuse can be very upsetting if we do not have a clear understanding of why we became a victim. We may have thoughts such as 'Why did they pick on me?', 'Did I do something wrong?', or 'Is there something about me that encourages attack?'

Aggressive and threatening behaviour usually has a strong emotional impact. Part of the process of coping with challenging behaviour is managing the emotional response following the events. It is natural to feel emotions involving hostility and resentment towards people who have threatened your own self-esteem or well-being. Part of the process of coping is to recognise your own feelings and to work out a way in which your emotions can be used positively to increase your confidence in coping with challenging situations.

While some people feel anger at being threatened, other people may experience feelings of guilt. You may have thoughts such as these: 'Perhaps I handled it badly – I'm sure there is something I could have done better. Perhaps I'll never be any good at this work.' It is easy to convince yourself that experts can predict and control everything and that highly skilled people never have difficulties. But not all incidents can be prevented. Self-blame can sometimes be useful if it leads us to reflect on our behaviour, but the problem with self-blame is that it can lead to the negative emotional conclusion that you cannot improve anything because you are a 'bad' or 'incompetent' person.

The desire to punish people who have threatened us, or the desire to punish ourselves, needs to be understood as one expected result of emotionally charged experience. So it is important to acknowledge the feelings you have, but then to move on and do something constructive that might improve your self-confidence and self-esteem. Sometimes professional counselling is needed in order to help people achieve this difficult task.

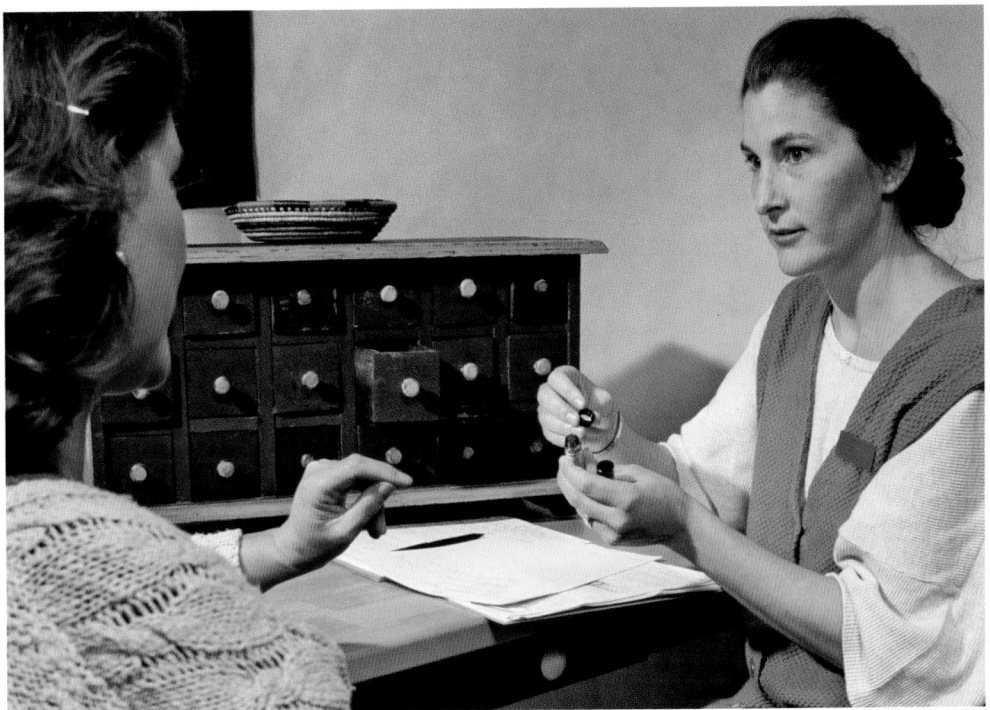

Talking through the experience with a trusted colleague or supervisor may help you to cope with your reactions

For many people it will be important to be able to understand and interpret why the event may have happened in the way that it did. Theory has a role to play in helping us to understand events. If we can understand some of the ways in which frustration, and feeling out of control, can cause people to become aggressive, this may help us to think positively and be able to improve self-confidence as a result of an experience.

CASE STUDY: Understanding an aggressive incident

Rick works in a day centre for people with learning difficulties. He runs cookery classes for small groups of service users. He enjoys very good relationships with all the service users in the centre and usually there is a very happy and supportive atmosphere in the teaching sessions.

Two weeks ago, however, Rick reported an incident where one of the service users – Tia – became very aggressive and threatened to stab Rick and other service users with a knife she was using. Although Rick was eventually able to talk Tia into putting down the knife, and although no one was injured, the incident keeps going through his mind. During his supervision session, Rick discusses the incident as follows.

Rick The thing that is really worrying me is I still don't know exactly what happened. I mean – I thought we had a good understanding. She has always responded well to me before but on this day she didn't. I don't know what triggered her to become so aggressive. Did I do

Continued

CASE STUDY: Understanding an aggressive incident

	something wrong – was I just not observant enough? I mean, it should be possible to stop these things happening, right? So I must have not been paying attention. It scares me to think that this could happen again and I don't know how to stop it.
Supervisor	What possible reasons might there have been for Tia to become aggressive?
Rick	Well, that's the problem – I don't know, but I ought to know.
Supervisor	Why do you think it's your responsibility to know this?
Rick	Well – an expert would be able to spot these things and prevent aggression, wouldn't they?
Supervisor	No, perhaps they wouldn't. No matter how much you have studied and no matter how much experience you've had, you have to remember that people are immensely complicated. Most of the time we can guess what other people are feeling – perhaps we can often predict how they might react – but there will always be situations that even the most expert person cannot predict. We can't know exactly what Tia was thinking, and we can't know what was happening in terms of her physical state. The thing was that you handled the situation very effectively. You stayed calm, you made things safe for the other service users and you used your understanding of Tia to help her cope with the emotion she was feeling. So, well done – perhaps that's all anyone can do!

1 *Rick is using reflective skills (see Unit HSC 33) in order to try to find an answer to the problem of preventing aggression. How effective is the supervisor in helping Rick to develop his skills?*

2 *Why does Rick believe that there must be a simple answer to preventing aggression?*

3 *The supervisor confronts Rick with the idea that all we can do is to develop skills for managing situations – we cannot always predict how people will behave. Is Rick's supervisor right about this?*

4 *If Rick feels confident that he can manage aggressive behaviour, how will this help him in working with service users in future?*

It may also be important to understand that sometimes you can become a target for 'displaced anger'. For example, some people have had the experience of being dominated and bullied by authority figures. Sometimes this might start with an authoritarian father in the family, and as a result some people view all authority figures as their enemies. Even though you may have been calm, assertive and friendly, your behaviour may have been viewed with suspicion. One long word that the other person did not understand may have been interpreted as an attempt to dominate and belittle them. The abuse or aggression you experienced may not really be a direct consequence of the word you used, but the word may have acted as a trigger for pent-up anger and aggression – perhaps harboured for many years.

Discussing a stressful event with your supervisor can be very helpful, provided your supervisor is able to support you to make sense of what happened. It is important to be able to resolve your understanding of incidents of aggression without needing to resort to blaming others, or holding on to the feeling that either you or the people who have wronged you are in some way 'evil' and should be punished.

Income and expenditure budget chart			
Step 1 – Income	**Weekly**	**Monthly**	**Yearly**
Salary/wage			
Other income			
Pension			
Jobseeker's allowance			
Income support/pension credit			
Housing benefit			
Other benefits			
Interest on savings			
Total			
Step 2 – Expenditure			
Mortgage or rent			
Second mortgage/secured loan			
Council tax			
Water rates			
Ground rent			
Repairs & maintenance charges			
Buildings insurance			
Contents insurance			
Gas			
Electricity			
Telephone			
Food			
Clothing			
TV rental and licence			
Prescriptions			
Health insurance			
Car tax and insurance			
Petrol/diesel			
Car repairs and servicing			
Public transport			
School uniforms, etc.			
Holidays			
Credit cards and loans			
Maintenance payments			
Contribution to pension			
Reserve for emergencies			
Regular savings			
Total			
Step 3 – Financial position			
Total income			
Total expenditure			
Financial position			

Research using the Internet

When you are supporting an individual to manage his or her financial affairs, you may need to research information on financial matters. The Internet is a fast and easy tool for finding up-to-date specimen costs, such as for insurance premiums or a comparison of the charges made by utility companies. It also offers a wealth of information on matters such as benefits, investments, taxation and pensions. But remember that the Internet is unregulated and not every source of information can be relied upon.

Be sure you access information only from the websites of dependable, well-established organisations and from universities, charities and government departments, and that you always cross-check any information you are using for financial planning with an appropriate source.

You may find government reports and the results of inquiries, or university research reports, have relevant information that you could follow up.

Managing debts

If you are supporting an individual who is in debt, you should encourage him or her to enlist the support of an experienced debt counsellor. These can be contacted through the Citizens Advice Bureau, welfare rights advice centres and local money advice centres. However, just as it is useful for you to know the general outline of the way the benefits system works, it is helpful if you understand the steps that a debt counsellor will take in order to resolve an individual's problems.

Citizens Advice Bureaux can provide the support of an experienced debt counsellor

The first thing that a debt counsellor will do is establish the nature of the debts an individual has. Debts are divided into **priority debts** and **non-priority debts**. Priority debts include:

- mortgage or rent
- council tax

Case study: Entitlement to benefits and allowances

Mrs Flanagan has lived alone since her husband died 25 years ago. She keeps her small house neat and clean and has always been very independent, doing all her own shopping, gardening and cleaning. She has a son in another part of the country who visits about twice a year. She is friendly with her neighbours and attends her local church where she has a wide circle of friends.

Mrs Flanagan has been finding it increasingly difficult to manage on her single state pension. Until she was admitted to hospital for investigations for a bowel condition she had no idea that she may have been entitled to additional support. Despite having a wide circle of friends and contacts in the local church she never considered discussing her personal financial circumstances with anyone outside her family, and on the occasions when she saw her son she did not want to burden him with discussions of her financial affairs. It was a passing comment she made to one of the support workers at the hospital, about the hospital food being a considerable improvement on what she could afford at home, that prompted a few further questions to Mrs Flanagan, and led to the discovery of the small pension she was receiving.

Mrs Flanagan was advised about what she could claim and was supported to make a claim for pension credit. As a result she received additional income, bringing her weekly income to the guaranteed minimum level. This made a huge difference to Mrs Flanagan, who was now able to run her home and do her shopping without the worry and anxiety she had endured for many years.

1 *What steps could have been taken to provide Mrs Flanagan with this information much earlier?*

2 *How would you organise an information campaign for people like Mrs Flanagan?*

3 *What sources would you target for information to help people such as Mrs Flanagan?*

Completing the paperwork

Benefit claim forms are usually very long. Great improvements have recently been made in the way they are structured to make them much simpler to understand, but it is often the length of these forms that inhibits people from filling them in.

Completing the forms is not as arduous as it appears, however, as for the vast majority of people large parts of the forms will not need to be filled in. These are the sections asking about investments, property owned and other sources of income. Even so, the mere appearance of the form makes some people feel unable to complete it.

Filling in a form may not be as difficult as it looks

The Benefits Agency has a system for filling in forms over the telephone and sending them to individuals for checking and completing. This is a valuable service for many people and ensures the information is entered in the correct places on the form. However, where individuals do not want to do this by telephone you may be asked to assist them in completing application forms.

Don't just take over the filling in of the form; an individual may only need you to check that it has been completed correctly. One important point to note when checking is to make sure that an individual with no income or no savings writes 'none' in the appropriate boxes.

You may need to make sure that an individual making a claim fills in the form legibly. This is important, as any difficulty in making out the details may cause a delay in processing the claim. Also, the information could be interpreted wrongly and the wrong decisions made in respect of benefit. If an individual's writing is not clear, you will need to handle this with tact and care – a person may well be offended if you imply that he or she cannot complete a form legibly.

Where individuals have literacy problems, you could offer either to assist or to complete the form on their behalf. Another approach is to encourage them to use the telephone application line.

You may have to deal with individuals who refuse to complete the whole form because they feel it is too long and complex, or because they are not willing to provide all the information the form asks for, such as information about their savings. You can only explain to them what the consequences will be of not providing that information. For example, if the individual is claiming a means-tested benefit the claim will not be considered unless all financial information is provided. The individual must be aware of the consequences of actions in order to make an informed decision about whether to pursue the claim for a particular benefit by providing all the necessary information.

Potential difficulties

If you are aware that an individual is attempting to make a deliberately fraudulent claim for a benefit or is making a deliberate attempt to mislead an agency providing a benefit about his or her circumstances, you must:

- explain that you cannot support this action and that you will be unable to assist in making the claim
- make it clear that if the individual persists in making a fraudulent or misleading claim you will have to record the matter and report it to your agency
- report the matter to your line manager, who will advise you on your agency's policy.

Active knowledge

Obtain a copy of a benefits claim form (such as a form for income support). Check it through to familiarise yourself with its style.

Methods of collecting benefits and allowances

Payment into bank accounts

You will need to discuss and agree with the individual the best way you can support him or her in collecting any benefits or allowances. State benefits and many other payments from private pensions or employer pensions are now paid directly into people's bank accounts. If the individual does not have a bank account, it may be helpful if you can explain the value of having one, and give him or her information on how benefit is paid directly into it and how relatively easy it is to access it.

Advise individuals on safer places to keep money

Where help may be needed

Where payments are being made directly into a person's bank account, you should encourage him or her to check bank statements regularly to make sure that all the necessary payments are being recorded in the account.

If you are dealing with money for individuals in residential care, your work setting will have its own form for recording money received on behalf of each individual and how much is spent. This will have to be recorded carefully, as will any payments made into bank accounts held in the individual's name.

Ways of ensuring individuals keep their money safe

In settings where you are working with vulnerable adults, whether they are residential or in the individual's own home, it is necessary to discuss with them the safety and security of any money they have. Many vulnerable people who continue to live in their own homes, particularly those who are elderly or with disabilities, are at high risk of being robbed if they keep cash in the house. Elderly people are more likely to keep large amounts of cash and you should discourage this wherever possible. They and their money will be much safer if they can be persuaded to keep it in a bank, building society or post office savings account.

In a residential setting there will be arrangements for the safe keeping of individuals' valuables and money. They should be encouraged to use this facility rather than keep money in their room, handbag or wallet. If an individual refuses to use the safe-keeping facility provided by a residential establishment, it is likely that he or she will be asked to sign a disclaimer form to acknowledge being offered the facility and having chosen to take care of valuables personally.

If you are aware of any cash being lost or stolen from an individual you must immediately report the loss – to your line manager if you are in a residential setting or to the police if you are working with individuals in their own homes. People are likely to be distressed by the loss of valuables, so you will need to offer them a lot of support during this time.

Evidence indicator

Check out the system for recording individuals' finances in your workplace. Think about how it could be improved, in terms of ease of use and its suitability. If you feel improvements could be made to update, simplify or extend it, try designing a new system of recording.

When you have done this you may want to discuss it with your line manager. It might be brought into use in your work setting! Keep your notes as evidence for your portfolio.

This will be easy – you know what old people are like – they keep their cash stashed away in the house because they don't trust banks

Older people who keep large sums of money in the home risk being robbed

Supporting individuals to make payments

Much of what you need to do in supporting individuals to make all the payments they need to make will depend upon the circumstances of the individual. You could be carrying out this type of task for a wide range of service users, each with varying levels of ability to manage their own financial affairs.

Establishing the level of help and support

One of the best ways to work out with an individual the level of support required is to look at the reasons why he or she needs assistance to make payments. It could be because the person is:

- specifically unable to make payments
- confused and too forgetful to make payments
- unsure what payments have to be made
- unlikely to be able to motivate himself or herself to make payments on time
- unable or unwilling to recognise the importance of making payments.

Once you have established the reasons why support and help are needed, it is much easier to agree the level of support. For example, if your assistance is required simply because someone is physically unable to write a cheque or to walk to the post office or the bank, it may be quite sufficient for you to write out cheques (if your employer's policy permits this) or to take things to the post office. There may be no need for you to assist with the process of identifying payments due or to become involved in any financial planning.

If an individual is unable to make payments because he or she is confused or unable to recognise the importance of making payments when they become due, he or she may be happy for you to become involved at a more detailed level in financial budgeting and planning.

Be aware at all times, however, that feeling unable to manage their own financial affairs may have an adverse impact on the self-esteem and self-image of individuals. Your work should always make it clear that the individual is the decision-maker on his or her own money issues, and that your role is only to assist in practical matters. Also, make sure individuals know you are conscientious about respecting confidentiality in all financial dealings, so that they do not feel their financial affairs have become 'public property'. Your professionalism, your understanding and the reassurance that their affairs are being taken care of in an efficient manner will do much to help individuals accept the situation while retaining their self-confidence.

Encouraging individuals to be self-managing

One of the keys to working effectively with individuals, whatever your role, is that you should always encourage them to take as much active responsibility as possible. Never assume that they will always require assistance at the level you currently provide. You should always review progress and wherever possible, either because their condition has improved or because they have learned from working with you, individuals should resume as much responsibility as possible for their financial planning, budgeting and payments.

Keys to good practice: How to encourage self-management

✓ Always begin by asking the individual to do as much as possible of the preparation for planning finances. Find out what the individual can do first, then support where necessary.

✓ Always check with the individual on everything you are doing, and ask 'What do you think?'

✓ Always make a regular review time for any financial support plan. This could be three or six months, depending on circumstances. At this stage you should review your level of support to see if the individual's needs have changed.

✓ If you notice changes between reviews, for example bills that have not been paid which the individual used to deal with, follow this up and make changes if necessary.

✓ If the individual is beginning to take more interest in financial matters and makes suggestions, check whether he or she would like to take more responsibility and reduce your involvement.

Range of payments

We all have our own range of payments to make, either regularly or as one-offs. While everyone has different financial demands made on their income, there are some types of payments that are more likely to occur for most of the individuals you work with.

When you are looking at the payments that need to be made by particular individuals, you should first ask them to identify, if they are able, which payments they need to make. It can be helpful to have a written checklist to try to make sure no payments have been forgotten. The list on the next page is a suggestion only, and it will obviously vary for each individual.

An individual may have trouble remembering all the payments that have to be made

Checklist of payments

Regular payments (which could be weekly/monthly/annually):

Rent	Mortgage
Food	Council tax
Heating and lighting	Water
Repair or maintenance charges	Telephone
TV licence	TV/video/satellite rental
Catalogue payments	Credit card payments
Insurance	Hire purchase or loan payments

Occasional payments:

Clothes	Furniture
Entertainment	Holidays

Such a checklist can be used for any individual, and additional items may be included to meet each person's circumstances. Once you have identified all the payments individuals need to make, you should discuss with them which payments they wish you to undertake and which payments they will continue to undertake themselves.

At this stage it is also useful to discuss methods of payment with the individual and to look at the advantages and disadvantages of the range of payment methods available.

Methods of making payments

The following table lists the different methods of payment for goods and services and the advantages and disadvantages of these.

Method	Advantages	Disadvantages
Cash	Easy for those who receive wages or benefits in cash. Easily understood. Allows people to see their exact financial position.	Safety – keeping cash represents a serious burglary risk. Loss – cash is easy to lose, particularly if an individual is confused or forgetful. Inconvenience – cash cannot be sent in the post, so cash payments have to be made directly or through a bank, and this can mean having to make arrangements to visit the offices or the bank of the payee.

Continued

Method	Advantages	Disadvantages
Cheque	Convenient – can be sent by post. More secure than cash. Generally accepted (with a cheque guarantee card).	Requires bank account. Can incur considerable bank charges. Becoming less used with the advent of electronic bank cards. Cheque book can be lost or stolen. Cheques can be misused.
Electronic bank card, e.g. Switch or Delta	Convenient, generally accepted. Easy to carry and use. Easy to stop if stolen.	Requires bank account. May confuse some individuals. Can be stolen and misused.
Standing order – set up by individual	Regular payments made by bank. No action needed by individual. Makes payments directly.	Requires bank account. Individual needs to remember to alter it if payments change. Incurs bank charges.
Direct debit – set up by payee	Regular payments made by bank. No action needed by individual. Makes payments directly.	Requires bank account. Can incur bank charges.
Credit card	Enables payments to be made even if individual is temporarily short of money. Convenient.	Can accumulate large amounts of debt. Has higher interest charges. Is easily stolen and misused. Not accepted for all types of payment.
Telephone/ online banking	Can be used by individuals who have bank accounts with access via telephone/Internet/satellite TV. Can be used without leaving the house. Does not require any permanent arrangement. Is safe and secure.	Only available to those with the necessary hardware and level of technological understanding to use the equipment.

Cash can be a convenient method of payment, but it raises safety and security issues

Active knowledge

Carry out this exercise on your own personal finances. Make a list, as above, of all the payments you make and the range of methods you use to pay. Check which items you pay using which methods. If you include grocery and general household shopping, you may find that the balance of methods you use alters. Similarly, if you look at methods of payments for large items you may also find that this alters the balance of the different types of payments you use.

Review the payment methods that you currently use and consider whether you could benefit by changing any of them in order to save on charges or interest rates, or to improve convenience or safety.

Case study: Support with making payments

Rosa has suffered from severe depression since the birth of her third child, now one year old. Her other children are aged two and four. Her husband left six months ago as he felt unable to cope with her depressed state. Rosa has been receiving medication from her GP for her depression, which helps to some extent, but she finds it very difficult to cope on a day-to-day basis.

She was referred for support by her health visitor who was concerned about her motivation and her seeming lack of ability to organise the basic requirements of living for herself and her three children. Rosa had neglected to pay the mortgage on the house, not because of a lack of income but because she had not been motivated to make the required arrangements to transfer the payments after her husband left. She was being threatened with repossession of the house, and as she had not paid recent utility bills there were various threatening letters from the companies.

A support worker began to work with Rosa and her family, and following agreement with her made arrangements for all of her utility bills and mortgage payments to be made via direct debit. The support worker negotiated with the building society to extend the mortgage period by the missing six months and negotiated with the utility companies to allow Rosa to pay off the excess amounts over a period of time.

1 *What could have been the consequences for Rosa and her family had the support worker not begun to work with them?*

2 *What alternative ways could have been used to resolve Rosa's problems?*

3 *What other effects might you reasonably expect to see from the improvement in Rosa's financial situation?*

4 *What skills would the support worker need to have used in order to improve Rosa's circumstances?*

Ways of recording payments made

All payments made for any goods or services require a receipt. It is important that you encourage individuals always to obtain and keep receipts for any payments made. By doing this it will always be possible to resolve any disputes about the timing and amounts of payments, and it avoids confusion over which bills have and have not been paid.

Good grief! I've really got to sort this out. I just don't know where I am with all this stuff.

Individuals may need to be advised how to organise their records for easy access

If you are making a payment on behalf of an individual, it is essential you obtain a receipt and keep a copy in the individual's case notes or receipts file. This protects you and the individual if any question about the payment is ever raised.

Receipts can come in a range of formats. Payments made via a bank will be recorded on a bank statement, so an individual receipt will not be needed. However, payments made by cheque, debit card or credit card need a receipt of individual transactions, which are kept until the transactions appear on either the bank statement or credit card statement. This makes it easy to identify any unexpected or unauthorised payments. Also a transaction receipt helps to resolve any dispute over the transaction.

Receipts should be maintained in a system where they are easily accessible – the sideboard drawer does not qualify as easily accessible! A simple filing system where receipts are categorised as utility bills, food, TV licence, clothing, holidays, etc. may be the easiest way of ensuring they can be located when they are needed.

Receipts should not be kept indefinitely, and the system will have to be maintained. Receipts for any item under guarantee should be kept at least for the life of the guarantee. Other receipts should be kept until the payment shows on a statement of that particular account.

Many individuals do not see the importance of keeping receipts or may forget where they have put them or lose them. You should try to obtain agreement to set up a system which they can use or, if that is beyond what they feel able to undertake initially, ask them to hand receipts to you until they become more familiar with the system. This is likely to prove the most effective way of recording financial transactions.

Ways of dealing with potential conflicts

You may be faced with a dilemma if individuals ask you to make payments in certain situations or tell you they intend not to make certain payments. This could involve:

- making payments for illegal items
- making payments for items of which you personally disapprove
- deliberately avoiding making payments that are due.

Illegal payments

If someone asks you to make a payment that you know is illegal, for example to pay for stolen goods or any other illegal items, then you should explain that it will not be possible for you to assist and that it is inappropriate for you to be asked to undertake this. If you become aware that an individual is involved in criminal activity you must report this to your line manager and follow your agency's policies and procedures.

Payments of which you disapprove

On the other hand, an individual may ask you to assist with making payments for an activity that is perfectly legal but is in conflict with your own beliefs and values. An example would be if you were strongly opposed to gambling and someone asked you to place a bet with a bookmaker on his or her behalf. In such a case you must be sure that you do not allow your own beliefs and values to influence the level of service you provide for the individual. However, your agency will have a policy on whether you may make payments to place bets or purchase alcohol. It will be important to check your agency's policy on any issue that you are uncomfortable with.

Put it on Starlight Express in the 3.30 for me, mate

You cannot allow your beliefs and values to affect the service you provide to individuals

The intention not to make payments

If individuals advise you that they are not going to make payments for goods or services or to meet their legal requirements, then you can find yourself in a difficult position. For example, someone could advise you during the budgeting process not to include an allowance for a TV licence as he or she does not intend to purchase one, despite having a TV. In this situation you should advise the individual of the consequences of his or her actions and the levels of fines that are imposed on those who fail to purchase a TV licence.

You are not, however, in a position to insist on a certain action or to override the individual's wishes. You are only able to advise and ensure that any decisions made about failing to maintain or make payments are based on an informed choice. You should record this information and advise your line manager accordingly, and explain to the individual that you are doing this.

You should never actively condone or encourage people to avoid making payments that they are required to make. Be careful that you do not give the appearance of encouragement by failing to comment. You do have a responsibility to ensure that an individual is informed of the potential consequences of any actions.

Reviewing effectiveness

Regular reviews will be necessary to monitor the effectiveness of the support provided to individuals in connection with their financial affairs. The methods and services selected may not continue to be appropriate, either because of a change in the individual's needs – individuals may need more or less help as time goes on – or because of a change in circumstances.

It is important that, at the outset of providing support for individuals, you work with them to decide how and when to review the effectiveness of the procedures put in place. At each review you will need to consider:
- what is working well
- which procedures need to be changed in order to improve support
- what is not working and needs a complete rethink
- any support that is no longer appropriate and can be discontinued
- any further support that has become necessary.

You will need to support the individual to identify the specific changes that need to be made, and work with the individual and other key people to make sure the agreed changes are implemented as soon as possible. Then make sure that future reviews are planned for an appropriate date.

Test yourself

1 List the different ways in which payments can be made.

2 Identify four reasons why people may refuse to claim benefits to which they are entitled.

3 How would you support an individual who felt it was impossible to complete a benefit claim form, because it was so long?

4 Why is it important regularly to review the effectiveness of the methods and services individuals use to manage their financial affairs?

Useful contacts

Benefit Enquiry Line (BEL)
Telephone: 0800 88 22 00
Fax: 01772 23 89 53
E-mail: Bel-Customer-Services@dwp.gsi.gov.uk
National, free telephone advice and information service on benefits for people with disabilities, their carers and representatives. It is available from 8.30 am to 6.30 pm weekdays and from 9 am to 1 pm on Saturdays. People who are deaf, hard of hearing or speech impaired and who use a textphone can call the benefits enquiry line free on 0800 24 33 55. Advisers can send out forms and give advice but they have no access to personal records. The Department of Work and Pensions has a helpful website: www.dwp.gov.uk

Counsel and Care
16 Bonny Street
London NW1 9PG
Advice line: 0845 300 7585
General enquiries: 020 7241 8555
E-mail: advice@counselandcare.org.uk
Website: www.counselandcare.org.uk

Provides free and confidential advice to older people, their carers and professionals. The advice line is available from 10 am to 1 pm on weekdays. Fact sheets on topics ranging from benefits to care homes are also available. Useful fact sheets include 'Choosing a care home: fees and funding', 'Paying care home fees: community care' and 'Community care and the NHS: a guide to making a complaint'.

Help the Aged
207–221 Pentonville Road
London N1 9UZ
Telephone: 020 7278 1114
Seniorline: freephone 0808 800 6565
E-mail: info@helptheaged.org.uk
Website: www.helptheaged.org.uk

Gives advice by letter or telephone on topics affecting older people, such as benefits, community care and home safety. Useful information sheets include 'Paying for residential care' and 'Residential care: problems with local authority funding'. Seniorline is available on weekdays from 9 am to 4 pm.

Help the Aged Care Fees Advisory Service
St Leonard's House
Mill Street
Eynsham
Oxford OX29 4JX
Freephone: 0500 76 74 76 (9–5 weekdays)
Fax: 01865 733 001

Citizens Advice Bureau
The National Association of Citizens Advice Bureaux
Myddelton House
115–123 Pentonville Road
London N1 9LZ
Website: www.citizensadvice.org.uk
Information and advice website: www.adviceguide.org.uk

HSC 345 UNIT TEST

1 Where can information be obtained about benefits and allowances? Name at least three sources.

2 What would be the general areas of benefit that you would advise people over 60 to consider?

3 What would be the general areas of benefit that you would advise families on a low income to consider?

4 What would be the general areas of benefit that you would advise people with a disability to consider?

5 What are the ways in which the benefit system can contribute to the independence of individuals?

6 Write about the ways in which you feel the benefit system could be improved.

7 What other sources of income could you explore for an individual, other than state benefits and allowances?

8 What are the advantages and disadvantages to an individual of using direct debits to pay bills?

Move and position individuals

The level of assistance individuals need in moving and achieving the correct position can vary from needing help to get out of a chair to being completely dependent on others to move them, to turn them over and to alter their position in any way, for example if they are unconscious or paralysed.

When individuals require this degree of care it is essential that they are moved and handled in the most sensitive and safe way. Safe procedures are also vital for you as a worker, and the people you work with – the commonest causes of people being unable to continue to work in health or social care are that they suffer injuries, usually back injuries, from lifting and moving individuals. It is possible to minimise the risk to yourself, to colleagues and to individuals for whom you provide care by following the correct procedures and using the right equipment.

The first element is about preparing the equipment, environment and individuals themselves for being moved. In the second element you will need to ensure that you know the way to carry out the move correctly and safely, and offer all the support people need.

What you need to learn

- Health and safety measures
- Working with the individual to be moved
- Suitable clothing and equipment
- How to encourage independence
- Equipment for moving and handling
- Methods for manual moving and handling
- Recording and passing on information.

HSC 360a Prepare the equipment, the environment and the individual for moving and positioning

Health and safety measures

As you learned in Unit HSC 32, all aspects of health and safety are covered by legislation. Moving people safely is no exception. The Health and Safety Executive guidance states:

1. The Manual Handling Operations Regulations 1992, which implement the Manual Handling of Loads Directive, came into effect on 1 January 1993 under the Health and Safety at Work Act 1974, and enable UK legislation to implement a European Community Directive on the manual handling of loads. They apply to all manual handling activity with a risk of injury.

2. The Regulations impose duties on employers, self-employed people and employees. Employers must avoid all hazardous manual handling activity where it is reasonably practicable to do so. If it is not, they must assess the risks in relation to the nature of the task, the load, the working environment and the capabilities of the handler and take appropriate action to reduce the risk to the lowest level reasonably practicable. Employees must follow appropriate work systems introduced by their employer to promote safety during the handling of loads.

Ensuring safety for both yourself, your colleagues and the person being moved is the joint responsibility of you and your employer.

The HSE provides guidelines about weights that can be safely lifted – these are very general guides and are not a substitute for a risk assessment, because many factors can affect the risks in each situation.

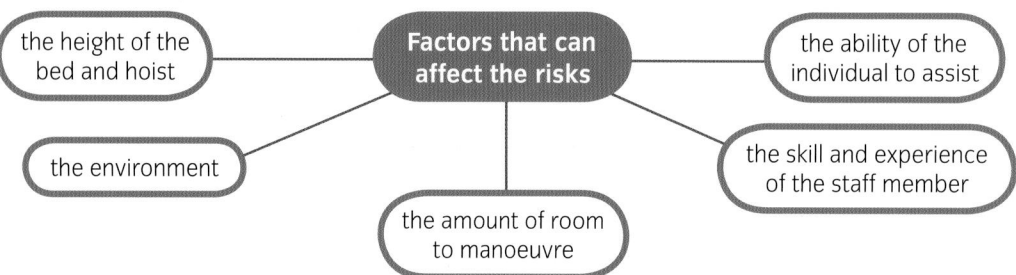

the height of the bed and hoist

Factors that can affect the risks

the ability of the individual to assist

the environment

the skill and experience of the staff member

the amount of room to manoeuvre

The HSE guidelines are based on moving inanimate objects, not people – who can move, wriggle, complain and co-operate (or not)! But these guidelines are useful in showing how little weight can be lifted safely, and serve as a useful warning to THINK RISK.

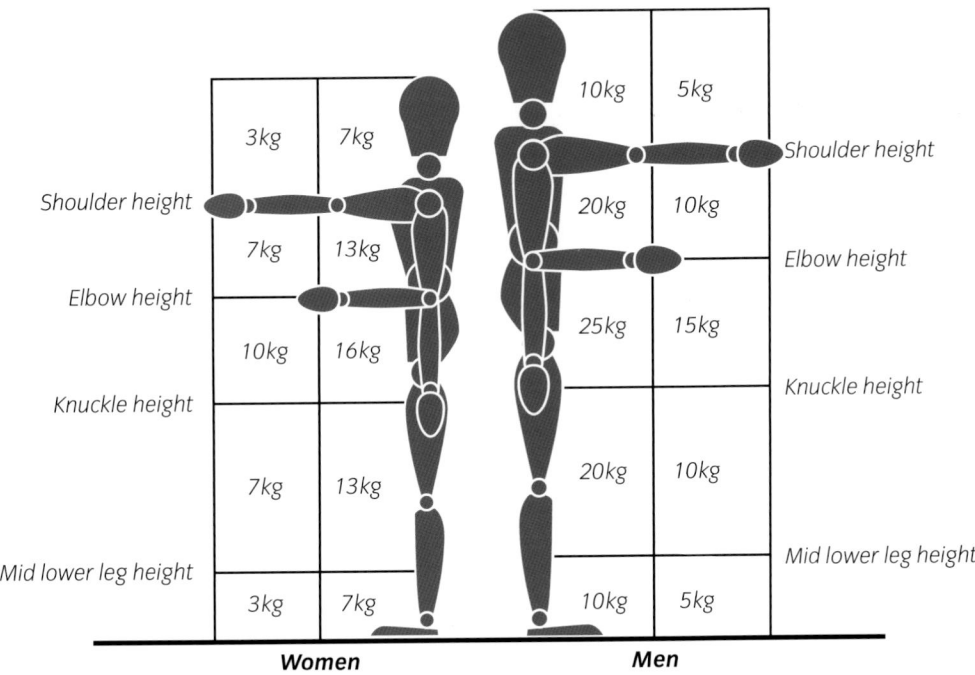

Women — Men

(diagram guideline weights)

Shoulder height — Women: 3kg, 7kg — Men: 10kg, 5kg — Shoulder height

Elbow height — Women: 7kg, 13kg — Men: 20kg, 10kg — Elbow height

Knuckle height — Women: 10kg, 16kg — Men: 25kg, 15kg — Knuckle height

Women: 7kg, 13kg — Men: 20kg, 10kg

Mid lower leg height — Women: 3kg, 7kg — Men: 10kg, 5kg — Mid lower leg height

Each box in the diagram above shows guideline weights for lifting and lowering.

Observe the activity and compare to the diagram. If the lifter's hands enter more than one box during the operation, use the smallest weight. Use an inbetween weight if the hands are close to a boundary between boxes. If the operation must take place with the hands beyond the boxes, make a more detailed assessment.

The weights assume that the load is readily grasped with both hands, and the operation takes place in reasonable working conditions with the lifter in a stable body position.

Any operation involving more than twice the guideline weights should be rigorously assessed – even for very fit, well-trained individuals working under favourable conditions.

There is no such thing as a completely 'safe' manual handling operation. But working within the guidelines will cut the risk and reduce the need for a more detailed assessment.

Source: HSE 1998

Infection control

Hygiene is also an important safety factory to consider, as the possibility of cross-infection is always present when you are working closely with and handling individuals. See Unit HSC 32 for advice on infection control, especially how to ensure your own hygiene – including standard precautions and the correct procedure for washing your hands.

How to assess risks

As you will remember from Unit HSC 32, your employer has a responsibility under health and safety legislation to examine and assess all procedures which take place in your working environment involving risk. All risks must be noted, assessed and steps taken to minimise them as far as possible. Your employer is responsible for providing adequate equipment for such tasks as moving and handling individuals who require assistance.

There are responsibilities on both the employer and the employee. The process of reducing risk is a joint responsibility – you must make your contribution in the interests of your own safety and that of your colleagues, as well as that of the person you are moving.

The employer's duties are to:

- **avoid** the need for hazardous manual handling as far as is reasonably practicable
- **assess** the risk of injury from any hazardous manual handling that can't be avoided
- **reduce** the risk of injury from hazardous manual handling, as far as reasonably practicable.

Employees' duties are to:

- follow appropriate systems of work laid down for their safety
- make proper use of equipment provided to minimise the risk of injury
- co-operate with the employer on health and safety matters; a care assistant who fails to use a hoist that has been provided is putting himself or herself at risk of injury, and the employer is unlikely to be found liable
- apply the duties of employers, as appropriate, to their own manual handling activities
- take care to ensure that their activities do not put others at risk.

Remember

The process of reducing risk is a joint responsibility of employer and employee.

Look after your back

Ideally every workplace should have, or have access to, a Back Care Advisor (BCA). These are people who are trained in manual handling and are able to provide expert advice to managers, manual handling supervisors and to members of staff who are involved in manual handling.

You must ensure that you follow the information provided by the BCA for your workplace, and take every opportunity to attend information and education events to make sure you are up to date on manual handling techniques and policies.

If you are supervising other staff, or have a responsibility for training, you must ensure that staff are trained and regularly updated. The health and safety officer in your workplace should also be able to provide up-to-date information regarding moving and handling.

Active knowledge

Find out who the BCA is for your workplace, and ask him or her when the next education sessions are planned.

Checklist

1   Is individual weight-bearing?

    Yes ☐

    No ☐

2   Is individual unsteady?

    Yes ☐

    No ☐

3   What is the general level of mobility?

    Good ☐

    Poor ☐

4   **a** What is the individual's weight? _____

    b What is the individual's height? _____

    c How many people does this lift require? _____

    (Work this out on the scale devised by your workplace)

5   What lifting equipment is required?

    Hoist ☐

    Sling ☐

    Trapeze ☐

    Transfer board ☐

6   Is equipment available?

    Yes ☐

    No ☐

7   If not, is there a safe alternative?

    Yes ☐

    No ☐

8   Are the required number of people available?

    Yes ☐

    No ☐

9   What is the purpose of the move? _____

_____

10 Can this be achieved?

    Yes ☐

    No ☐

A checklist for assessing risks before moving an individual

The risk assessments your employer carries out are, however, general risks for your work environment. Each time you move or lift any individual, you too must make an assessment of the risks involved in carrying out that particular manoeuvre. Even if you have moved this individual every day for the past six months, you should still assess the risks on each occasion before you put anything into practice. If you are acting in a supervisory capacity, you must ensure that staff are fully aware of the procedures they are required to follow.

No two lifts are ever the same – there are always some factors that are different. These factors could be to do with the individual and his or her mood or health on that particular day; they could be about the environment; or they could be about you and your current physical condition.

You should run through the same checklist each time before you carry out any activity which involves you in physically moving a person from one place to another. A suggested checklist is shown on the previous page. You may need to adapt it to fit your own place of work and the circumstances in which you work.

Any changes in an individual's condition may influence the moving and handling procedures required. These should always be recorded in the care plan and a new risk assessment carried out whenever necessary.

This checklist system is best remembered as TILE – Task, Individual, Load, Environment. You should carry out a TILE assessment each time you move a service user.

You need to consider the environment carefully when you are assessing risk. You should take into account all of the following factors.

- Is the floor surface safe? Are there wet or slippery patches?
- Are you wearing appropriate clothing – low-heeled shoes, tunic or dress that has enough room to stretch and reach?
- Is the immediate area clear of items that may cause a trip or a fall, or items that could cause injury following a fall?
- Is all the equipment, both to carry out the lift and in the place to which the individual is to be moved, ready?
- Does the individual have privacy and can his or her dignity be maintained during the move?
- Is there anyone you could ask for help, for example a colleague, a porter or member of the ambulance service?

Remember

T	Task
I	Individual
L	Load
E	Environment

Working with the individual to be moved

Make sure you wash your hands and ensure your own hygiene before and after moving individuals. Bacteria on bed linen can easily be transferred from individual to individual unless care is taken to observe infection control procedures.

Consult the care plan and assess any immediate risks to individuals. If there is a risk you cannot deal with, seek advice from the appropriate people.

Muscles are attached to the bony skeleton. They work like hinges or levers –
they pull and move particular joints. When a muscle contracts (gets shorter),
it pulls a joint in the direction that it is designed to move. Pairs of muscles
move antagonistically; that is, when one contracts, its opposite number
relaxes to allow movement. Muscles can become slack and make movement
slower and more difficult, but when muscles are regularly used they are toned
and easy to move.

Types of joint

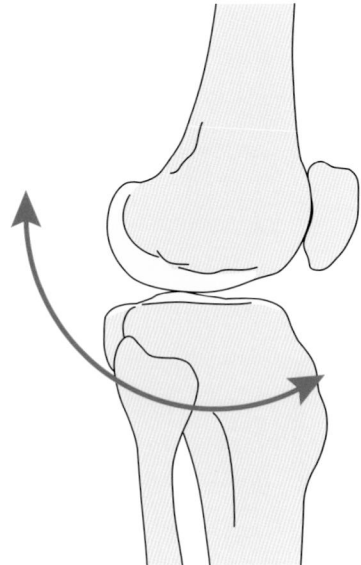

The knee is a hinge joint

- **Hinge joints**, e.g. the knee or elbow joint, can straighten or bend in the
  same way as a door hinge opens or closes.
- **Pivot joints**, e.g. the vertebrae in the neck, allow movements from side
  to side.
- **Saddle joints**, e.g. the thumb, allow back-and-forth and side-to-side
  movements, but rotation is limited.

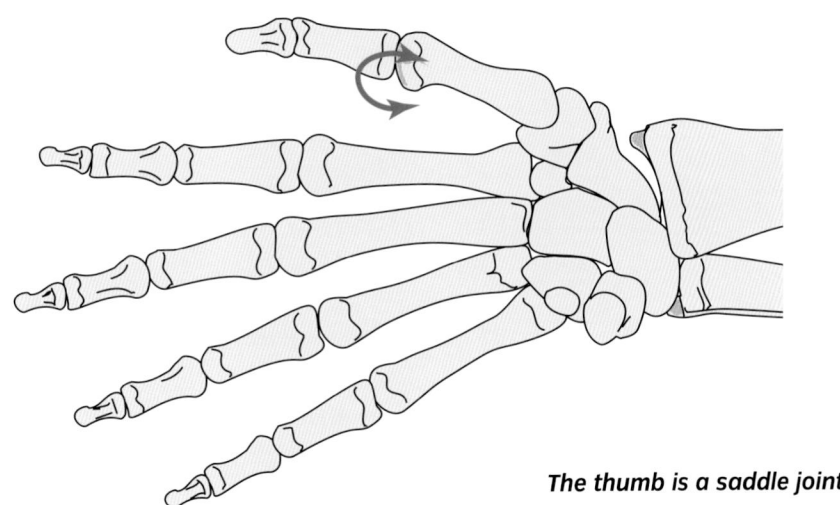

The thumb is a saddle joint

- **Ellipsoidal joints**, such as the joint at the base of the index finger, allow bending and extending, and rocking from side to side, but rotation is limited.
- **Gliding joints** occur between the surfaces of two flat bones that are held together by ligaments. Some of the bones in the wrists and ankles move by gliding against each other.
- **Ball and socket joints** are the most flexible free-moving joints, e.g. the shoulder and hip.

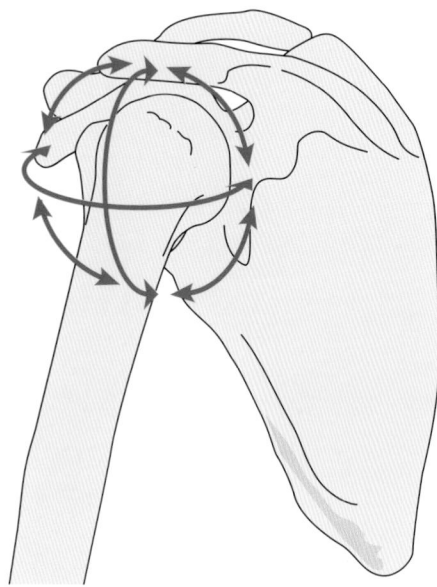

The shoulder is a ball and socket joint

How the knee moves

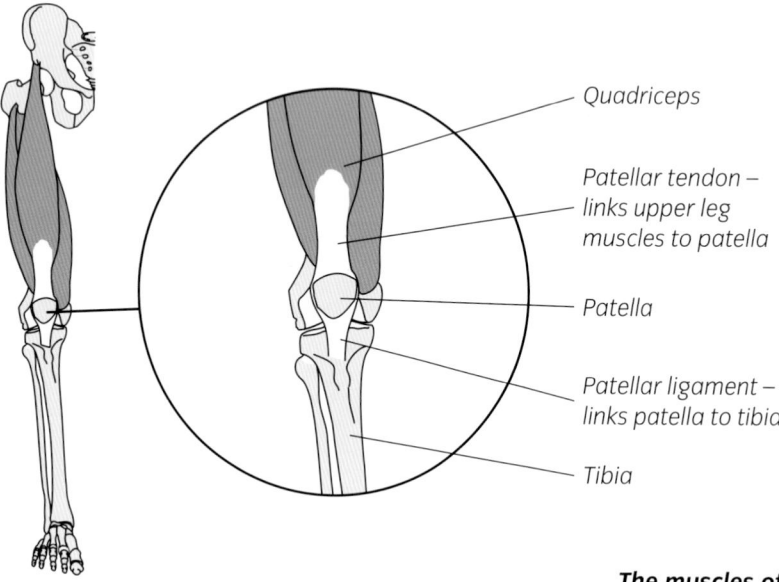

Quadriceps

Patellar tendon – links upper leg muscles to patella

Patella

Patellar ligament – links patella to tibia

Tibia

The muscles of the knee

The muscles responsible for moving the knee run from the upper to the lower leg. Those in the front of the upper leg (the quadriceps) pull on the tibia (lower leg bone) to straighten the leg. The muscles at the back of the upper leg make the knee joint bend.

How the upper arm moves

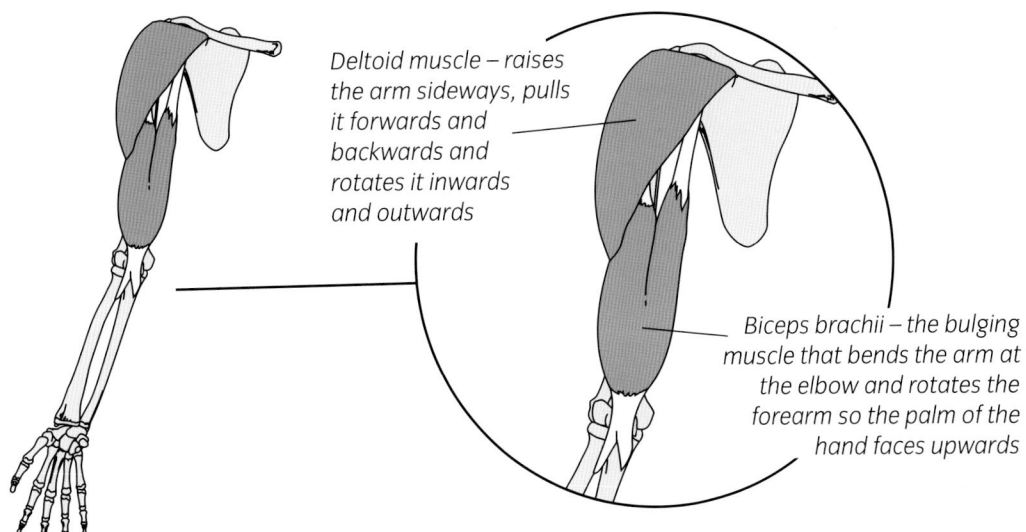

Deltoid muscle – raises the arm sideways, pulls it forwards and backwards and rotates it inwards and outwards

Biceps brachii – the bulging muscle that bends the arm at the elbow and rotates the forearm so the palm of the hand faces upwards

The muscles of the upper arm

The large muscles in the upper arm work together to raise and bend the arm. The most powerful arm muscle is the biceps brachii. If you bend your arm up and down, you will feel the biceps working.

Improving particular conditions

Exercise can be specifically designed to improve particular conditions. A physiotherapist would make an assessment and design a particular programme for an individual with this in mind. Some examples are shown below.

- Following a stroke, an individual will often have weakness in a limb or the whole of one side of the body. A mobility activity will be designed by a physiotherapist to work on strengthening the areas weakened by the stroke.

- Following surgery to replace a hip joint, an individual may have muscle weakness of the whole of the leg because of lack of exercise caused by osteoarthritis. In addition, he or she will have pain and stiffness following surgery. The key to recovery and regaining full use of the joint will be the plan devised by the physiotherapist.

- Many people who use wheelchairs may have special mobility activities to ensure that their muscles remain active as far as possible, and to promote their general fitness levels.

Explaining the move

Once you have carried out all the necessary assessments in an individual case, you should explain carefully to the individual exactly what you intend to do and what his or her role is in contributing to the effectiveness and safety of the move. This will vary according to the person's ability, but nonetheless most individuals will be able to participate to some extent.

Even where individuals are unconscious or appear to have no understanding of what is going on, you should still explain exactly what you are doing and why you are doing it and what the effects will be. We have a limited understanding of what a state of unconsciousness means to the person experiencing it; however, it is acknowledged that individuals who appear to be completely unconscious may be able to hear what is going on around them. Every individual has the same right to be treated with dignity and respect and to have procedures explained rather than simply having things done to him or her by care workers who believe that 'they know best'.

Each stage of the proposed move should be explained in detail before it is carried out, and it is essential to obtain the individual's consent before you move or handle him or her in any way. If you move an individual without his or her consent this could be considered to be an assault. So you should always be sure that you are carrying out the individual's wishes before you commence any move.

Keys to good practice: Preparing for moving and handling

✓ Wash your hands and ensure you are wearing suitable clothing and footwear.

✓ Check the care plan and assess risks to the individual and to yourself before starting any move.

✓ If the risk assessment states that more than one member of staff is required to perform the procedure, ensure that one or more colleagues are available to assist you.

✓ Remove potential hazards and prepare the immediate environment.

✓ Ask the individual about the best way of moving, or assisting, him or her.

✓ Explain the procedure at each stage, even where it may not be obvious that you are understood.

✓ Explain how the equipment operates.

✓ Check that you have the agreement of the person you are moving.

✓ Stop immediately if the individual does not wish you to continue – you may not move a person without his or her consent.

Never be tempted to drag an individual up the bed or chair, instead of ensuring that he or she is properly moved. Dragging someone can cause friction and break the skin, promoting the development of pressure sores, especially on the sacrum (the bottom of the back) and heels.

Suitable clothing and equipment

Your clothing

The type of clothing you wear when you are moving individuals is very important. It can make the difference between carrying out a procedure safely and doing it with difficulty and possible risk of injury. Footwear should be supportive and flat, with soles that grip firmly.

Recommendations in respect of uniforms are that dresses should have a pleat in the skirt and in the back, and a similar pleat in the sleeves. These are to allow space so that you do not find that your own movements are restricted by your clothing, possibly forcing you to move in an awkward way. It may be necessary, for example, to place one knee on a bed. This is impossible if you are wearing a straight skirt, or at least very difficult to manage at the same time as maintaining dignity – yours, not the service user's!

If you are in a situation where you do a great deal of moving and handling, it is a good idea to wear trousers, with a tunic top that has plenty of room in the sleeves and shoulders to allow free movement. Your employer should have carried out a risk assessment and ensured that the clothing that is provided for you to wear is appropriate and complies with current best practice and requirements in terms of moving and handling.

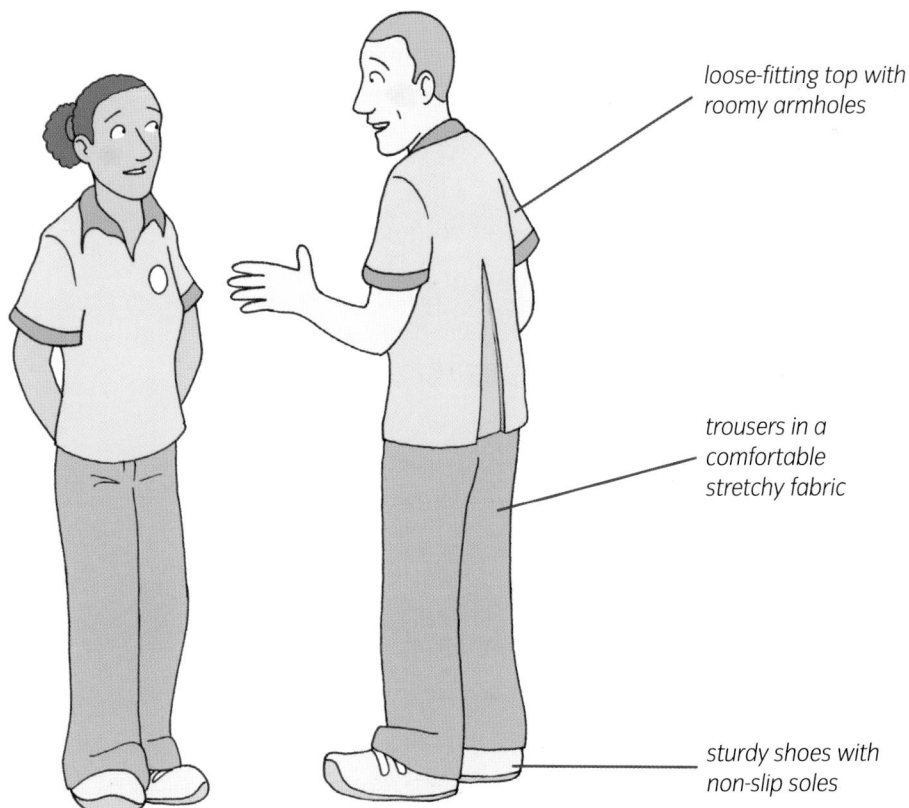

loose-fitting top with roomy armholes

trousers in a comfortable stretchy fabric

sturdy shoes with non-slip soles

Work clothing should allow for free movement when handling individuals

Equipment

The use of equipment is covered by the Lifting Operations and Lifting Equipment Regulations (LOLER) 1998.

LOLER covers risks to health and safety from lifting equipment provided for use at work. LOLER requires that equipment is:

- strong and stable enough for the intended load
- marked to indicate safe working load
- used safely: the equipment's use should be organised, planned and executed by competent people
- subject to ongoing examination and inspection by competent people.

Hoists, slings and bath hoists are covered by the regulations. The regulations state that lifting equipment should be thoroughly examined by competent people at least every six months in the case of equipment used to lift people, and at least annually in the case of other equipment.

In your work you may use many different types of equipment, including several types of lifting and moving equipment. It is important that you check every time you use a piece of equipment that it is safe and that it is fit for use for that particular individual.

If you do find equipment has become worn, damaged or appears to be unsafe in any way, you should immediately stop using it, label it as being damaged, take it out of service and report it to your supervisor. You must do this even if it means having to change your handling assessment for the individual you were about to move. You should also ensure that other members of staff are aware that the equipment should not be used until it is repaired or replaced.

Under no circumstances is it acceptable to take a risk with equipment that may be faulty. It is better that the individual waits a little longer for a move or is moved in an alternative way rather than being exposed to risks from potentially unsafe equipment.

Make sure that you have read the instruction manual for each piece of equipment you use. It should give you a safety checklist – make sure you follow it, and that colleagues do so too.

Also make sure you seek any assistance you need in order to carry out a move correctly using any type of equipment. Safety procedures will specify how many workers are needed for each type of move.

Evidence indicator

Find out the procedure in your workplace for reporting faulty equipment. Check whether there is a file or a book where you need to record the fault. You may only need to make a verbal report, or you may have to enter the details of the fault into a computer. Make sure that you know what the correct procedure is, and make notes on it for your portfolio.

How to encourage independence

There are many ways in which an individual can assist and co-operate with care workers who are handling or moving him or her. It is important that this is encouraged and that individuals are not made to feel as though they are simply being transported from place to place 'like a piece of meat'. Co-operation from the individual is invaluable, both for maintaining his or her own independence and for assisting those who have to carry out the move. For example, you may be transferring an individual from a bed to a wheelchair. The first part of the process – getting to the edge of the bed and sitting on it – may well be possible for the individual to accomplish if he or she follows a correct set of instructions, rather than having to be moved by care workers.

Any independence that can be achieved is vitally important in terms of the individual's self-esteem and sense of well-being. A person may be able to transfer himself or herself from a wheelchair to a chair, to a car seat or into bed, either by the use of transfer boards or by simply being able to use sufficient upper body strength to slide across from chair to wheelchair, and vice versa, once the wheelchair arm is removed.

You may be able to use self-help techniques when an individual needs a bed pan. Rather than having to be lifted manually, he or she can be encouraged, with some simple instructions, to bend the knees and raise the bottom to allow the bed pan to be slid underneath him or her.

Techniques like this involve the active co-operation of the individual. Obviously they are not suitable for use where individuals are unable to co-operate, either because of their state of consciousness or because they have almost total paralysis. Some individuals may not be able to co-operate for emotional reasons – they may lack the confidence to make any moves for themselves because of fear of falling or fear of pain or discomfort. Where the plan of care has identified that the individual is capable of co-operation in moving and handling, this should be gently encouraged and any reasons for his or her reluctance to co-operate should be discussed with the individual.

Where there is any conflict between the individual's wishes and health and safety issues, it is important that these are discussed and that you explain to the individual that you must abide by statutory regulations to protect him or her, as well as yourself and your colleagues. Every attempt must be made to reach a compromise so that you can carry out any moving and handling procedure according to the guidelines, while meeting the needs of the individual as closely as you can.

Good preparation is the key to a successful move or transfer. Where the individual and the worker are working together, there is likely to be maximum safety and minimum risk, pain and discomfort.

Remember

If an individual can achieve any part of a move or transfer, with or without support, this will be invaluable both for the individual's self-esteem and in assisting the care worker.

CASE STUDY: Planning a move

Shireen is the care worker for Mrs Gold, who is 80. Shireen needs to move Mrs Gold from a bed into a chair. Mrs Gold is only able to assist a little as she has very painful joints and is unable to bear weight. She weighs 16 stones (101 kg).

1 *What would you expect to see in Mrs Gold's care plan in respect of moving procedures? Give reasons.*

2 *What factors should Shireen take into account before starting to move Mrs Gold?*

3 *What should Shireen say to her?*

Test yourself

1 Name three factors you would take into account when assessing the risk of carrying out a move.

2 In what sort of situations would you consider asking an individual to move himself or herself across the bed?

3 What type of clothing is most suitable for carrying out lifting?

4 What steps should you take if you have concerns about the safety of equipment?

HSC 360b Move and position the individual

You are ready to begin the moving and positioning of individuals when you have consulted the care plan and individuals themselves (where possible), assessed all risks and applied precautions for infection control.

Equipment for moving and handling

A wide range of equipment is available, and technological advances are being made continuously in the field of medical equipment. But regardless of the individual products and improvements that may be made to them, lifting and handling equipment broadly falls into the following categories:

- hoists, slings and other equipment, which move the full weight of an individual
- equipment designed to assist in a move and to take some of the weight of an individual, such as transfer boards
- equipment designed to assist the individual to help himself or herself, such as lifting handles positioned above a bed to allow individuals to pull themselves up. This category also includes grab handles, raised toilet seats, patient hand blocks and lifting-seat chairs.

Care workers in a hospital or residential setting should never have to lift or move service users without the necessary equipment. This is sometimes more of a problem in community settings, where it may not be easy to use equipment in the service user's home, or the equipment may not be available.

The Disability Rights Commission has highlighted the issues in relation to the human rights of people with disabilities. They argue that if disabled people are unable to live in the way they wish because of a 'no lifting' policy – for example, some people have had to remain in bed because no equipment was available to move them, or they did not wish to be moved using equipment – then the agency refusing to provide the care is in breach of both the Human Rights Act 1998 and the Disability Discrimination Act 1995.

There is no direct instruction in the Manual Handling Regulations not to lift, but they do state that all personnel should 'avoid hazardous manual handling where reasonably practicable', and many organisations, particularly within the NHS and social services, instruct their employees not to lift at all. However, guidance from the Health and Safety Executive – 'Handling Home Care', 2002 – states that while all risk assessments must be undertaken and equipment used wherever possible, 'no lifting' policies are likely to be incompatible with service users' rights.

The NHS 'Back to Work' guidance also states that 'no lifting' is a misleading term as it is often used to mean that lifting most, or all, of a service user's weight should not be undertaken. In no circumstances, however, should the service user or care worker be put at risk.

Evidence indicator

Check the policy in your workplace about moving individuals against the Health and Safety Executive and NHS guidelines. Does it conform? If not, what changes need to be made? Check the most recent information from the Disability Rights Commission. Are all the staff you are responsible for aware of this? Make notes on your findings for your portfolio.

If you need to move someone manually in order to change his or her position or to provide assistance, you should follow the principles of effective manual moving and handling.

- Risks must be assessed *every time*.
- The procedures should be well-planned and assessed in advance. Technique rather than strength is what is important.
- The procedure should be comfortable and safe for the individual – creating confidence that being moved is not something to be anxious about and that he or she can relax and co-operate with the procedure.
- The procedure should be safe for the workers carrying it out. A worker who is injured during a badly planned or executed transfer or move is likely in turn to injure the individual he or she is attempting to move. Similarly, an individual who is injured during a move is likely to cause an injury to those who are moving him or her.

Team work

Most moving and transfer procedures, whether manual or assisted, are carried out by more than one person. If you are to work successfully as part of a team, you need to follow some simple rules.

- Carry out a risk assessment.
- Decide who is going to 'shout', or lead the manoeuvre.
- That person will check that everyone is ready.
- He or she will say '1-2-3 lift' or '1-2-3 move'.
- Everyone must follow the count of the person who shouts.

Remember

The interests and safety of the individual and the workers are so closely linked that you must consider them both together.

Transfer

If you are assisting an individual to transfer from a bed or chair to a wheelchair, this can be done with one person providing assistance to steady the person as he or she uses the transfer board, provided that there are no complicating factors such as an individual who is particularly heavy or tall, or who has serious disabilities. In that case, the person should be moved using a hoist or a turntable.

Rolling or turning

If you need to roll or turn someone who is unable to assist, either because of paralysis, unconsciousness, serious illness or confusion, you should:

- follow the care plan and risk assessment
- carry out the procedure with at least two workers
- roll the person using a transfer sheet or board, or use the bottom sheet to roll the person onto his or her side (make sure the sheet is dry and intact!)
- support the person with pillows or packing.

When the person needs to be turned again, remove the pillows, lower him or her onto the back and repeat the other way.

Overcoming 'pyjama-induced paralysis'

One of the key factors in a safe handling policy is to encourage people to help themselves. There is a great temptation for people to believe that they can do far less than they are capable of. This is often encouraged by staff who find it quicker and easier to do things rather than wait for people to help themselves.

If you encourage individuals to make their own way out of bed, for example, they need to follow the simple set of instructions shown on the next page.

You may wish to encourage an individual to roll over in the bed, rather than having to be manually rolled by a care worker. This could be necessary to allow for a change of bedding, a bed bath or to change clothes. The instructions for achieving this are quite simple, and can be carried out by all but the most severely ill or disabled individuals, as shown on the next page.

10	322, 332
11	332
12	321, 341
13	347
14	321, 329, 341
15	321, 329, 341
16	334, 339, 347
17	321, 329, 341
18	335
19	332, 334
20	329, 332, 339, 346

HSC 360
Values

1	356
2	356
3	356, 363

Legislation and organisational policy and procedures

4	352, 366, 373
5	352, 366, 373
6	353
7	354

Theory and practice

8	356, 363, 374
9	352
10	356, 358
11	354, 374
12	367, 372, 373
13	359
14	363
15	356, 363
16	363, 367
17	356, 358
18	376
19	368
20	366
21	352, 364, 372
22	364, 372
23	356
24	374
25	352, 369
26	364
27	352, 369
28	354, 356
29	372
30	376
31	376